Logos
logo, identity, brand, culture

identity, brand **culture**

logo, identity brand,
culture

identity, **brand,** culture

logo, **identity** brand,
culture

lo**go,** **identity,** br**and,** culture

logo, identity **brand,** culture

identity, brand, culture

logo, identity brand,
culture

Conway Lloyd Morgan

A RotoVision Book
Published and distributed by RotoVision SA
Rue du Bugnon 7
CH-1299 Crans-Pres-Celigny
Switzerland

RotoVision SA, Sales & Production Office
Sheridan House, 112/116A Western Road
Hove, East Sussex BN3 1DD, UK

Tel: +44 (0) 1273 72 72 68
Fax: +44 (0) 1273 72 72 69
E-mail: sales@RotoVision.com

Distributed to the trade in the United States by:
Watson-Guptill Publications
1515 Broadway
New York, NY 10036, USA

10 9 8 7 6 5 4 3 2 1

ISBN 2-88046-328-9

Book design by Wendy Williams

Production and separation in Singapore by ProVision Pte. Ltd
Tel: +65 334 7720
Fax: +65 334 7721

One of the great pleasures in creating and working on this series of books is the opportunity to talk to designers about their work, and this one has been no exception. Many busy people were willing to take time to explain their own work and discuss their approach to the tasks of creating logos and identities. As well as those who are mentioned or quoted in the text, I would particularly like to thank the following– Albrecht Bangert, Jim Brown, Debbie Cox, Patrick Farrell, Stuart Flanagan, Chris Foges, Jonathan Kirk, Dominic Lippa, Ann Marshall, Kathy Merriman, Kerry Morgan, Wally Olins, Lynda Ralph-Knight, Otto Riewoldt, Tim Rich, Thomas Riedel, Jocelyn Senior, Janet Turner and Sally Waterman.

Special thanks also go to Angie Patchell and Wendy Williams for their editorial and design work.

Conway Lloyd Morgan, London, August 1998

contents

Chapter 3
What is a brand? 74

Chapter 4
What is corporate culture and brand culture? 98

introduction
wearing the sign

'Cars today are almost the exact equivalent of the great Gothic cathedrals: I mean the supreme creation of an era, created with passion by unknown artists. Roland Barthes' essay on The New Citroën is included in Mythologies, his seminal text on products, design and society. He analysed the form of the 1950s Citroën DS (and lots of other things, from margarine to striptease) in social and perceptual terms, a semantic approach that he was among the first to devise, and which provided a spur to the development of issues such as brand management and product semantics. And the Citroën double vee logo is a key part of this analysis– the Citroën emblem, with its arrows, has in fact become a winged emblem, as if one was proceeding from the category of propulsion to that of spontaneous motion, from that of the engine to that of the organism.'

Barthes was right to focus on the Citroën logo (originally devised to reflect the angled intermeshing gears that were invented by André Citroen). Logos form a key part of the branding of a product or service, and of the corporate identity of a company or institution. Historically, logos predate branding and identity: the samurai with the banner of his daimyo fluttering behind his armour, the feathered headdress and body-painting of the Native American, and the Scot wearing a clan tartan, are all using external elements to signify their adherence to a set of values or concepts that are expressed visually. As do the football supporters with their faces painted in the team colours, the pensioners who put their modest purchases from a corner shop into a Harrods carrier bag or the

introduction
wearing the sign

teenagers who will only go to a disco in Versace jeans (even fake ones). The desire to identify oneself through emblems is an age-old human trait. At certain times in history it was a necessity, to establish rights or even to act as a form of public warning, as in the physical branding of criminals or the Nazis deliberate humiliation of Jews through the wearing of the Star of David.

In most modern societies displaying the wrong signs – or wearing the wrong colours – is a social gaffe not a life-threatening situation. But that does not mean that we are unaware of such signs, or even less that the manufacturing and service enterprises and companies that underpin, in a sense, modern societies are ignorant of the latent power of such signs. In fact, our understanding of such signs grows increasingly profound. To take the example of television advertising, twenty years ago it was dedicated to the selling of specific products and services: buy this soap, it said, or use this airline. Today the message is couched in different terms, whatever the specifics on offer. The consumer is not just asked to purchase but also to believe. Trust this soap with your body. This airline cares about your dreams.

This is not merely a change from hard to soft sell: it is part of a process of sophistication in which both the manufacturers' intentions and the customers' expectations have become more subtle, and in which, for the advertiser, convincing not only immediate purchasers but long-term potential purchasers has become cardinally important in maintaining market presence. As part of the same process the logo, a visual summary of the company's identity, has become the vehicle for expressing the philosophy and position of the company, become not just a means of identification – like a flag or banner – but a means of communication.

And so the design of logos, which a generation ago was simply about finding a neat visual solution to a name, is today a much more complex process, which feeds back into the internal culture of a corporation and outwards into the market's perception of its activities and offers. So the design process for logos has become inseparable from the concepts of branding and corporate identity – which in turn can be subsumed into a wider concept of corporate culture. At the heart of the idea of corporate culture is the idea of focus, that all the manifestations of a corporation, from the way its letters are worded or its annual reports illustrated, from the tactics of its softball team to the launch of a new product range, all elements are coherent with a specific view of what the corporation is and represents. So a failure of communication at any level threatens the totality.

These guidelines enable you and your suppliers to implement our identity easily and successfully

Always return items to the correct place in the binder after use

1 Our Design

Our Design
Overview

introduction
wearing the sign

The political validity or desirability of such a view of corporate culture is not here at issue: suffice it so say that the concept of the corporation as a dedicated single organism is the objective of much modern management teaching and practice. Whatever methods are used to create the final result, there is now little doubt that the logo or brand or marque or corporate identity plays a major role in creating and defining the corporate culture. For the logo designer, the consequences of this change are clear enough. The previously valid, visually derived solution is evidently inadequate, and what is needed are solutions sourced in an understanding of corporate values and aspirations. Once these are understood, a visual metaphor can be derived from them. As the case studies in this book show, this is a challenge that makes the designer's task more interesting, if also more difficult, and which endows the visual solution with a validity that goes beyond simple aesthetics.

So this is a change and a challenge which any and every designer should relish. It is clear that communication between people and peoples is essential for the continuation of peaceful society, and so that designers, as agents of communication, have a special social responsibility to express and maintain civic values. (If this seems exaggerated, look at the way design, along with other kinds of visual imagery, has been used to promote social ideas and political concepts over the last fifty years).

The practical consequence of the foregoing for a designer invited to advise on a new logo or branding or identity design is that whatever paper is received as a brief is likely to be inadequate in terms of the real problems to be considered. This is a drawback which can be turned into an opportunity, provided that it is understood that an intellectual appreciation has to precede a visual solution. Each case is different, as the studies of real design projects that follow show. But there are common features, or stages, through which each design progresses.

The first of these is understanding the brief, or more specifically the context of the brief. The designer's first task is to understand the values and aspirations of the client: this is the research phase. Next is the establishment of a dialogue with the client so that the visual ideas can be translated into concepts the client understands. This leads to the design solution, which has to be communicated to the client and through the client corporation. Since new identities are often the vehicle for changes in corporate culture and self-perception, this stage is often as important as the new visual material. Finally the design has to be implemented: a manual produced on paper or C.D-Rom, monitoring procedures set up, the purpose behind the design explained. And, with time, the design needs to be developed to respond to changing circumstances and requirements.

In this book we have presented the designs under headings that relate to this process: the background, the research phase, the solution, and added an assessment of each design. The designs have been grouped under logos, identities, brands and culture. But all show how designers today are using their skills in different forms of communication, and witness the complexity, challenge and enjoyment of working in the corporate field.

what

logo is a distinguishing mark for a company, a roduct, a service or a range of products or ervices from the same source.

A logo is unique to the company it represents, and can be protected legally as a trademark, trade name or registered mark.

A logo can be typographical, figurative, abstract or can be a combination of these.

A logo is one of the base elements in a corporate identity or brand identity.

A logo can be two or three dimensional, monochrome or coloured (though there is normally a two dimensional version for a 3D logo and a black and white version for a coloured one).

is a logo ?

A logo is the basic design equity owned by a company, alongside the company name. Say 'International Business Machines' and most people won't know what you mean. Say IBM and they will understand you in most languages! The IBM logo, designed by Paul Rand in the 1950s, has become a benchmark for quality in typewriters (IBM was a pioneer in developing electric and then electronic typewriters in the USA), in computer systems (the IBM company nickname 'Big Blue' comes, it is said, from the colour of the casings of the room sized computer systems it was installing for major corporations in the 1950s and 1960s, though another theory is that IBM executives always wore blue suits) and in personal computers. (The Open Systems Architecture and QDOS programming adopted by IBM became the standard on which the personal computer revolution of the last decade was built). The IBM logo has not been changed or modified since its introduction. It therefore stands alongside (and stands for) the qualities of reliability and efficiency which are the company's reputation. 'No-one ever got fired for buying IBM' is an old joke, but one which encapsulates the solidity of IBM's market position. It is a professional, business to business offer, based on mutual respect between partners. There is an interesting comparison here with the Apple Mac proposition, which is based on creativity and personal expression, rather than efficiency. Apple users have a fierce dedication to the product, seeing themselves as the computer revolutionaries, while in fact it was IBM's decision to base its PC on an open system that fuelled the computer revolution. While the IBM logo is part of a wider and very sophisticated corporate identity, which extends into corporate policy on architecture and sponsorship, the logo is the cornerstone of the company's image. It represents an asset of incalculable value, because it has been consistently maintained and protected over the years.

THE SAVOY

LAWYERS COMMITTEE FOR HUMAN RIGHTS

OXYGEN/ATOMIC SKI

TECHNIQUEST

CEARNS & BROWN

Be our guest

CLIENT

Savoy Hotel Group
London, UK.

DESIGNERS

Pentagram Design
London, UK.

PRODUCT/SERVICE

Prestiges hotels

the background

The Savoy in London is synonymous with luxury: it has a worldwide reputation for ordered elegance. I use to at one time travel to work on the same train as one of the banqueting managers. He would wear an immaculate grey, swallow-tail coat and striped trousers every day, even if he knew there was no function that day demanding his appearance, and he would be in his office all the time! The train was normally full of overnight arrivals at Heathrow, red-eyed and time-warped: he must have come as something of a surprise to them.

But established success is no guarantee of the future. The services guests expect from a luxury hotel change, and the origins and background of the guests themselves change as well, especially in an international meeting-point like London. One way of dealing with this change is by fragmentation: creating different areas in the hotel for different guest needs a busy brasserie for younger guests, a formal library bar for older ones, for example. The drawback to this approach is that it blurs the overall identity by trying to be too many things.

The Pentagram group was invited to advise the Savoy Group on the identity not only of the Savoy but of the two other luxury hotels they own in central London, The Berkeley and Claridge's. The principle question was should there be uniform group identity across all three, or should each have its own identity? If there was to be an overall identity, what should it be, or if there were to be individual identities, what should they be?

SAVOY

The designers were asked for a new identity for this famous hotel group: the typographic solution is
simple and direct, conveying the formal luxury that awaits guests in these very individual hotels with

THE BERKELEY

Claridge's

the solution

To answer the main question, Pentagram sought to analyse the advantages and disadvantages that would arise from a uniform style. In its view the advantages of a shared look (for example in advertising the hotels overseas) were outweighed by the disadvantages. Each hotel was different, in terms of location, architectural style and ambience, and in their market would lose out from being perceived as part of a chain. This answer is not surprising, but the advantage of analysing the situation was that it brought the designers and the management up to date on customer and public perceptions of the three hotels. In other words, though they had little doubt about the overall answer they would get, the detail in the answers was valuable for the next phase, designing the individual logos. For the three graphic identities, Pentagram realised that simplicity, or rather singularity, was the key to maintaining the standing of the hotels. Previous logos had either become very quickly dated, or had not been sufficiently well defined to operate under changing circumstances. Their proposal was therefore for a largely typographical solution in each case, the choice of typeface being determined by the character of each hotel. So the word Savoy was set in gold sans serif uppercase lettering, with the V larger than the rest. This is direct and eloquent, and a neat reference to the immense awning that greets the arriving visitor in Savoy Street. Claridge's, which is a rather more exuberant hotel, uses a busy serif typeface with some decorative scrolling. The Berkeley, in Knightsbridge, uses formal serif capitals.

By rights

CLIENT

Lawyers Committee
New York, USA
for Human Rights

DESIGNERS

Lippa Pearce
Richmond, UK.

PRODUCT / SERVICE

Human rights organisation

the background

In recent years charities and pressure groups have become aware of the need for clear visual identities to support their important work. This is partly a response to the growing visual awareness of society at large and the opportunity to present information visually, partly a response to the increasing range of public voices seeking the public's support for good causes, and partly a reflection of the growing international reach of many such issues.

Since 1978 the Lawyers Committee for Human Rights has sought to mobilise the legal community across the world to secure and promote the rights guaranteed by the International Bill of Human Rights. It now has a worldwide network of national groups, and actively lobbies international organisations and governments from its base in New York. The Committee works in conjunction with other groups such as the Witness Programme founded by Peter Gabriel, who also supports the Committee. Its constituency extends from national and international bodies to human rights activists, lawyers and, most importantly, the victims of persecution themselves. In 1996 the Committee decided that a redesign of its logo on a worldwide basis was needed, and asked the British firm Lippa Pearce to help.

The brief asked for a logo that would reflect in some way the core concerns of the Committee, would transcend national boundaries, and be appropriate for the range of different audiences . It would be used on stationery, signage, web sites and publications. The main constraint was that the logo should be carefully budgeted, and function in monochrome and in colour. The core concerns of the Committee are justice, fairness, equality and impartiality in the application of law, together with a respect for the principles of the International Bill of Human Rights.

'Design only works when it is based on a solid foundation of ideas, coherent, clear objectives and rational or emotional response triggers.' Harry Pearce.

LAWYERS COMMITTEE FOR HUMAN RIGHTS

The challenge was to find a symbol for an international human rights group that could be read visually in different cultures and still convey directly the concerns of the group. The logo had to be adaptable not only to letterheads but also for publications and information videos.

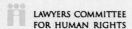

LAWYERS COMMITTEE
FOR HUMAN RIGHTS

Washington, D.C. Office:
100 Maryland Avenue, N.E.
Suite 502, Washington, D.C. 20002

Telephone (202) 547 5692
Facsimile (202) 543 5999
E mail WDC @ lchr. org

330 Seventh Avenue
10th Floor New York
New York 10001

Telephone (212) 629 6170
Facsimile (212) 967 0916
E mail NYC @ lchr. org

LAWYERS COMMITTEE
FOR HUMAN RIGHTS

Washington, D.C. Office:
100 Maryland Avenue, N.E.
Suite 502, Washington, D.C.
20002

Telephone (202) 547 5692
Facsimile (202) 543 5999
E mail WDC @ lchr. org

LAWYERS COMMITTEE
FOR HUMAN RIGHTS

L.Camille Massey
Director, Communications

330 Seventh Avenue
10th Floor New York
New York 10001

Telephone (212) 629 6170
Facsimile (212) 967 0916
E mail NYC @ lchr. org

the research

Lippa Pearce's approach to any design brief is to analyse the brief before starting the visual design process. In the case of the Committee, it looked at various factors. First came the existing identity, to monitor its strengths and weaknesses, and the identities of other pressure groups in the same field, to establish norms for the area. Then there were the needs of the organisation, requiring information about use of the new logo and the culture of the organisation, so that the new logo would speak in the right 'tone of voice', and the core values of the organisation and their meaning within and without the organisation, would achieve expression through the logo. Finally there was the environment where the identity would be put to work, and the expectations and requirements of that environment, consisting of the legal profession, government and the media.

Lippa Pearce used this research process to identify a number of different design routes and took these to a more developed visual for preliminary presentation to the client. Design routes allow the opportunity to explore different tones of voice and different creative solutions. Seven alternatives were studied for the Lawyers Committee, in part because of the need for a design to cross national and cultural boundaries. Two of these, chosen initially for further development, are shown here. One uses the visual idea of a bracket to link the support of the committee for human rights, another transforms the H of human rights into an icon of prison bars. These designs and the preliminary version of the final design were presented over a two day period to the Committee Board and to members and staff of the Committee. The executive director of the Committee then presented the selected design to groups of international activists: among the aspects discussed at all these stages was whether the design risked offending any national or religious sensibilities.

Analysing the alternative designs, it is clear that the bracket solution depended on reading a typographic device that might not be immediately apparent to all cultures. And if the title of the Committee was translated into foreign languages the layout of elements might change, so losing consistency. The prison bars approach also depended on reading the icon back into the letter H (again not appropriate in cultures where the roman alphabet is not the norm) and suggests a concentration on penal issues while the work of the Committee is wider in scope.

'The power of the symbol is its simplicity and grace – the basic concept of people working together towards a common goal.' Peter Gabriel, founder of the Witness Programme.

COLOUR CODING IS USED ON
STATIONERY TO DENOTE
DIFFERENT FUNCTIONS

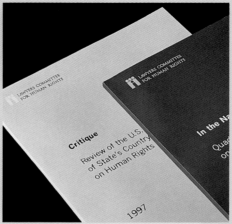

the solution

The final design can be read figuratively in a number of ways: an individual (in white) supported by a committee (in black), a witness before a jury, a leader fronting a team, even as a victim facing oppressors. In this way it addresses the concerns of all its potential audiences. As it is an abstract image it risks no offense, while having the independence and strength of a formal mark. Read typographically, it can be considered as based on the letter I, for international. It is deliberately classical, mature and serious, reflecting the tone of voice of the client. The four objectives Lippa Pearce set itself were authority, clarity, simplicity and longevity, representing the Committee's steadfast and direct purpose, its strength and maturity in the field, and its endurance and independence.

THE LOGO AS USED ON NEWSLETTERS, PUBLICATIONS AND SIGNAGE

the assessment

With the final logo design approved, the designers turned to the additional aspects of the design: the colour palette, associated typefaces and logos. The logo itself could be used as a positive or reversed symbol, and in and against a range of colours. These were defined in turn according to the objectives (red, for example, was excluded as a colour because of its political links, and the format and typography for newsletters and documents were to be clear, formal, businesslike and experienced). On letterheads, the logo appears in positive, with colours for different areas and functions, with the title of the committee on two adjoining lines in serif capitals. For publications, serif types were selected for their professional and human values, sans serifs for their clarity and legibility. The underlying principle was that directness of communication would contribute to the credibility and authority of the organisation. In the words of Camille Massey, communications director for the Lawyers Committee on Human Rights 'we are delighted to possess an identity that beautifully represents our organisation and will ultimately allow our human rights work to have a much greater impact worldwide.'

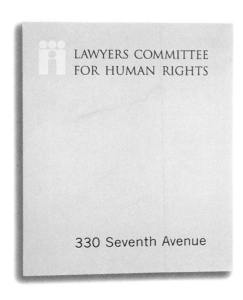

Inflating the image

CLIENT

Oxygen/Atomic Ski
Vienna, Austria

DESIGNERS

Rage Design
West Wycombe, UK

PRODUCT/SERVICE

Inline skates & accessories

the background

Inline skating is street cred at pavement level. It is about dexterity, about control, about style, about performance, about appearance. How you move is part of how you look, whether you are skating for fun, or for fitness. The appearance of the skates is part of their appeal, and is supported by accessories such as bags and caps, pouches and helmets, wristguards and gauntlets.

The branding, including the logo, of fashion/sports goods such as these is therefore critical to their market performance: the logos and marks represent an important design equity. So the Oxygen name in its encircling oval logo figures prominently on the skates themselves, on their packaging, and on accessories and printed material.

When Oxygen decided to extend its operations in Europe, it called in Rage Design, who already working on a number of sport/fashion accounts, for help with their printed material. 'One service we offer to a lot of our American clients', Rick Gaskell of Rage Design explains, is getting their ideas and images into a European context. It won't work today just to carry copy or presentations across from the USA to Europe or the UK directly. We need to redirect them for Europe, if you like. And so we are producing material in several European languages, for example.' He felt that the Oxygen logo needed some repositioning. 'Clearly it was an established brand and those values had to be respected and enhanced. But it was a little stiff in its appearance, which might have been a problem in languages such as German where the word would not be immediately known.'

An established brand in the sports/leisure field in one market (in this case the USA) may need to be modified slightly for European tastes, particularly as the products involved (inline skates) are aimed

THE AMENDED LOGO AS IT
APPEARS ON STATIONERY
AND BROCHURES

the solution

'We decided to put a bit of air into Oxygen,' Gaskell jokes. For the letterheads and cards for the new European company, based in Austria, Rage retained the existing logo, while printing it out of silver rather than out of white, and producing a second, inflated shadow version, which runs at an angle under the address panel, and is printed in a washed-out blue. The oval shape is also reinforced by a pattern of three blue ovals that form a graphic positioning feature on business stationery. Although visually soft, this change actually gives the brand more immediacy and attack. It positions it clearly in the tough world of youth culture and sports culture.

Do anything.
Go anywhere.
Just go for it!

This speeded-up version of the logo is also used as a graphic feature in the catalogue and other printed material, and as a visual backing element on packaging designs for smaller items. It is an adjunct to the main logo, not intended to compete with it at all, rather, in supporting the main name, giving it

Seeking science

CLIENT
Techniquest
Cardiff, South Wales, UK

DESIGNERS
HGV
London, UK.

PRODUCT/SERVICE
Science centre

the background

The redefinition of the museum is one of the most exciting aspects of late twentieth century culture. Rather than being just a static treasure house of objects and artifacts from the past, the modern museum has taken on a new role as a centre for learning, explanation and demonstration: an active rather than a passive role. This change has created the opportunity for new kinds of cultural or informational activity, not necessarily linked to holdings of rare or old objects, but with the same functions of informing and entertaining. The new Techniquest centre, created from the ruins of earlier industrial glory in the former docks area of Cardiff, is an example of the latter: a new space devoted to explaining the basics of science, for children – defined by Pierre Vermier, founder of HGV, as 'like with Tintin, children from the ages of seven to 77'.

The new Techiquest space is in a former warehouse, transformed by architects ORK into a white and open environment with an additional geodesic dome: it is the largest interactive science centre in the United Kingdom. HGV was asked to provide signage, graphics and a visual identity. The main constraint on the design was the budget, which was very small. The installations themselves, which demonstrated basic principles of science, especially physics, through physically interactive games, had been largely designed by the time HGV became involved, though it was able to work alongside the centre's staff in terms of colour and instructional material.

The main aim of the centre was 'to convey the questioning nature of learning about science', and the key terms derived from research both for the identity design brief and for the main installation design were colourful, flexible, and simple. 'We decided to use four primary colours - red, yellow, blue and green - in strong tones,' Vermier explains, 'as these were direct and fun, and so met the requirements of the brief'. A similar range of colours, together with white and transparent materials, was used in the interactive exhibits, so locking the two elements together.

An interactive science learning centre for young people needs to make an immediate visual appeal. The use of primary colours and a simple visual pun not only met the brief for the logo but also a

the **solution**

For the name Techiquest a direct visual pun was the solution: take the letter Q and substitute a ?, set at an angle. This was further refined by using standard sans serif capitals for the first six letters, and an extra-bold form of the same face for the balance. The question mark sits at the point of change, which in fact makes it easier to read as a Q, rather than otherwise. The angled question mark is also used as an independent element, for example on wrapping paper and packaging, and the colours are combined across the complete range of possibilities. 'There is no hierarchy of colours,' according to Vermier. 'The external signage is yellow on blue, as that has both high visibility, and works best with the colours of the external facade. But the director's business card uses red on green.'

THE LOGO ON THE EXTERIOR
OF THE BUILDING AND ON
A BASEBALL CAP

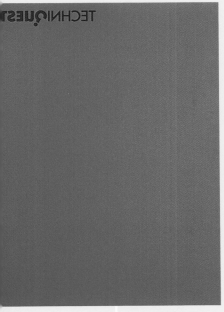

ALTERNATIVE COLOURWAYS
FOR THE USE OF THE LOGO
ON BADGES AND BROCHURES
AND THE QUESTIONMARK
MOTIF ON PACKAGING

the assessment

A number of complementary elements to the final solution have yet to be achieved because of budget: one such is a large exterior mobile, designed by Vermier, with circular discs advertising the centre and specific attractions or sponsored events. But otherwise the new identity and signage has been very well received, contributing to a doubling of attendance figures for the new centre. The success of the identity design stems from the simplicity of its elements and the verve with which they have been developed – even down to the coathangers in the cloakrooms being coloured and patterned to match the questioning design.

Move the meal

Cearns & Brown
Runcorn, UK.

DESIGNERS

Wolff Olins
London, UK.

PRODUCT / SERVICE

Food distributors & manufacturers

the background

Office canteens have been replaced in recent years by office catering, and schools, hospitals and other public services have increasingly been contracting-out catering services. So the market has become more complex and competitive. In the north of England, the old-established firm of Cearns and Brown has been supplying local kitchens and caterers with food products for many years. Half of its business was wholesaling for other manufacturers, half was selling its own products under the 'Countrywide' brand name. The result was that for some customers, the company was perceived as a food supplier, for others just a delivery service. To build a stronger market for its own brand, and to unify the two aspects of the business (which were not different in fact but were perceived as such) the company consulted Wolff Olins in London.

Wolff Olins realised when they researched the situation that the company needed to be seen as food specialists offering a service to a specific market: physical delivery was a key part of the business, but the assurance of product quality was far more important. What was needed was an image that would represent quality, and which could be modified to carry the concept of service. Furthermore, the company's clients were also food specialists -- caterers, chefs and kitchen staff. The people who would handle and use the products were professionals working in a busy environment. What they wanted was to put their hands on what they needed at the moment they needed it. Most of the several hundred products in the Cearns & Brown/Countrywide range were basics for the catering kitchen: tinned vegetables and fruits, pre-prepared sauces, pastas and rice. Thus the more direct the offer, the more successful it was likely to be, provided it spoke the right language to the user.

CEARNS&BROWN

The brief asked for a way of bringing the two strands of the client's business (food products and distribution) together in the eyes of their customers. A simple photographic approach with occasional

the solution

Wolff Olins borrowed the computer screen maxim - 'what you see is what you get.' The packs simply show what is inside them: tomatoes on the tinned tomatoes, beans on the beans, apples on the apple sauce. The products are shown in colour, the descriptions are on a uniform green band on a white background. The photography is straightforward: 'we had three months to create 700 packaging designs,' Lee Coomber of Wolff Olins jokes, 'so we didn't have time for a lot of retouching work.' Stylised photography would in any case have undermined the direct delivery implicit in the overall approach.

THE BASIC IMAGERY USED ON PACKAGING IS GIVEN A GRAPHIC TWIST FOR STATIONERY AND VEHICLE LIVERY

CEARNS&BROWN

Cearns & Brown
Whitehouse
Runcorn
Cheshire WA7 3BL

Tel: 01928 7155555
Fax: 01928 712582

CEARNS&BROWN

Cearns & Brown
Whitehouse
Runcorn
Cheshire WA7 3BL

Tel: 01928 7155555
Fax: 01928 712582

with compliments

Cearns & Brown Limited
Registered office: Whitehouse
Runcorn Cheshire WA7 3BL
Registered number: 123 456

CEARNS&BROWN

Whitehouse
Runcorn
Cheshire
WA7 3BL

Alexandra Parker
Marketing Co-ordinator

Tel: 01928 712345
Fax: 01928 714441

Cearns & Brown Limited
Registered office: Whitehouse
Runcorn Cheshire WA7 3BL
Registered number: 123 456

the development

For the vehicle livery, wit was the answer: take a tin or a bottle, furnish it with hand-drawn feet or wings, and use it large on the side of a white delivery truck or van. The result is highly visible, immediately links the delivery system to the product range, and has a light touch that suggests not levity but enthusiasm. Wit and humour in design are especially valuable in media that are by their nature ephemeral, such as television and press advertising, and often this is a more interesting approach than using the old war-horses of sex and luxury. In the context of identity design, humour is almost impossible to achieve, but a certain lightness (but not light-heartedness) can provide an antidote to the solid and sometimes overbearing expressions of corporate power that categorise some identities.

The running and flying tins and bottles are also used on some of the products that are 'customer-facing', such as sauce bottles and condiments, products that will come out of the kitchen and onto the serving area of a canteen or a pub counter. This makes a gentle link with a wider public, who may have seen a tin of tomatoes flying past on the motorway.

'Every time you see it, it works a little harder'
Lee Comber

REPETITION OF SIMPLE
ELEMENTS IS THE KEY TO
THE SUCCESS OF THE
DESIGN

CEARNS&BROWN
Horseradish sauce

2.2kg e

Best before end see lid

Ingredients
Horseradish, water, vegetable oil, sugar, skimmed milk powder, salt, spirit vinegar, dried egg yolk, stabilisers (guar gum, xanthan gum), colour (titanium dioxide), mustard flour, flavouring.

Store in a cool, dry place.
Once opened keep refrigerated.

Cearns & Brown
Whitehouse, Runcorn, Cheshire WA7 3BL

CEARNS&BROWN
Blue cheese dressing

2.1kg e

Best before end see lid

Ingredients
Vegetable oil, water, spirit vinegar, egg yolk, blue cheese solids, sugar, salt, modified starch, flavouring, mustard flour, stabiliser (xanthan gum), preservative (potassium sorbate), dried garlic, herbs.

Store in a cool, dry place.
Once opened keep refrigerated.

Cearns & Brown
Whitehouse, Runcorn, Cheshire WA7 3BL

CEARNS&BROWN
Tartare sauce

2.15kg e

Best before end see lid

Ingredients
Vegetable oil, water, dill pickle, spirit vinegar, glucose syrup, sugar solution, invert sugar syrup, egg yolk, thickener, modified starch, capers, salt, mustard flour, stabiliser (xanthan gum), parsley, dill oil.

Store in a cool, dry place.
Once opened keep refrigerated.

Cearns & Brown
Whitehouse, Runcorn, Cheshire WA7 3BL

CEARNS&BROWN
Barbeque sauce

2.6kg e

Best before end see lid

Ingredients
Water, tomato purée, glucose syrup, sugar solution, invert sugar syrup, spirit vinegar, salt, vegetable oil, emulsified sugar, spices, stabiliser, xanthan gum, dried onion, dried garlic, natural flavouring.

Store in a cool, dry place.
Once opened keep refrigerated.

CEARNS&BROWN
Mint sauce
Concentrated

2.3kg e

Best before end see lid

Ingredients
Water, spirit vinegar, sugar, mint, salt, colour (copper chlorophyll), riboflavin, stabiliser (xanthan gum), flavouring.

Store in a cool, dry place.
Once opened keep refrigerated.

Cearns & Brown
Whitehouse, Runcorn, Cheshire WA7 3BL

CEARNS&BROWN
English mustard

2.35kg e

Best before end see lid

Ingredients
Water, mustard flour, sugar, salt, wheat flour, citric acid, flavouring, spice, stabiliser (xanthan gum), natural colour (lutein), antioxidant (ascorbic acid).

Store in a cool, dry place.
Once opened keep refrigerated.

Cearns & Brown
Whitehouse, Runcorn, Cheshire WA7 3BL

CEARNS&BROWN
French vinaigrette

2.2kg e

Best before end see lid

Ingredients
Vegetable oil, white wine vinegar, water, Dijon mustard, sugar, salt, concentrated lemon juice, dried garlic, stabiliser (xanthan gum), black pepper, dried onion, basil.

Store in a cool, dry place.
Once opened keep refrigerated.

Cearns & Brown
Whitehouse, Runcorn, Cheshire WA7 3BL

the assessment

The base identity, expressed mainly through the packaging, as well as on letterheads and price lists, is simple and almost understated. It relies for its effect on regular contact, and the skill behind Wolff Olins, solution lies in the realisation that it is precisely in this way that the product will be seen and used by the eventual clients. Through regular use, the identity becomes, in Coomber's words, 'a style, or even a language, which is repeating gently the assurance of quality that is at the heart of the offer.' Such an approach would have been quite ineffective in a retail context, but here has considerable subtlety. It also binds the main offer to the parent company very effectively.

GRAPHIC WIT APPLIED TO
CUSTOMER FACING PRODUCTS
SUCH AS SAUCES

what is a corporate
identity?

A corporate identity is the visual statement of a company's role and function, a means of visual communication internally with its shareholders and employees and externally with its suppliers and customers.

A corporate identity consists of the logo and name (or names and logos) owned by a company together with the rules and guidance on how these are to be used, for example in printed material such as letterheads, catalogues and reports, in advertising, marketing and promotion, and on products and services.

A corporate identity often specifies which colours and typefaces are to be used with logos and names, and the desired relationship between them. Such colours and typefaces can also be among the design equities owned by the company.

A corporate identity is one of the base elements of a corporate culture. Robert Blaich, when he was head of the design section at Philips, the Dutch electronics giant, once pointed out to me that there was only one Siemens in the Munich telephone directory, so giving the company's Bavarian rival a head start in protecting its corporate name and identity. The name Philips, however, could not be protected as a word. So part of his task, as well as supervising the design of products ranging from razors to radio and lamps to laptop computers, was to create a corporate identity system that would link the product range with the company, and with the corporate values of innovation and quality, in the public mind worldwide. Since Philips' operations were truly global, consistency was essential, not only to protect the company's identity as compared to other businesses using, quite legitimately, the Philips name, but also to maintain Philips' position in a highly competitive marketplace. Blaich and his team at Eindhoven realised that the key to consistency was simplicity. Anything too complex was likely to fail, either through misinterpretation or through lack of attention to detail. They also wanted to be certain, at the time, that local printers anywhere in the world would have the necessary resources for printing letterheads or cartons or price lists for their local offices. So they adopted Univers, probably the most widely available typeface in the world, together with Times, as the corporate typeface, and 100 per cent cyan as the standard corporate colour, in which the Philips name would be printed. The second requirement for a consistent identity is rigor: the rules for every utilisation imaginable of the company name had to be considered and rules established. They therefore published a manual, running to some 600 A4 pages, setting out in detail the positioning, sizing and presentation of the Philips name (and any associated brand names or product names) in all situations on catalogues, on packaging, on products, in advertising in whatever media.

Today the same information is available electronically, on CD Rom or over the corporate intranet, as a system of templates for the use of the name. But the groundwork was essential. Only once this basis for coherence was in place could the more complex work of projecting the company's image be developed and sustained.

HONG KONG AIRPORT

BALLET-TECH

DUSSELDORF AIRPORT

VINOPOLIS

PHILIPS

Let's make things better.

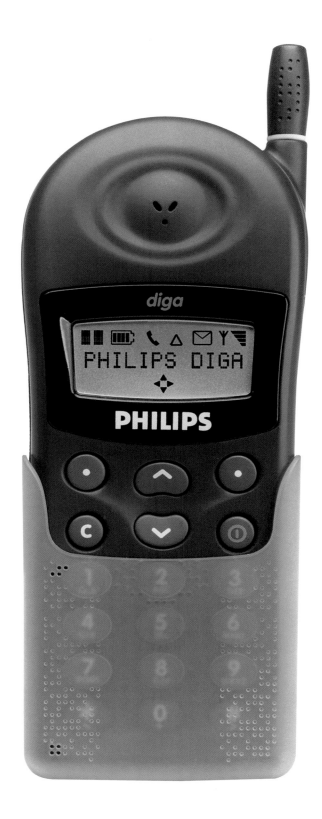

THE IDENTITY OF THIS
MOBILE PHONE COMES
NOT ONLY FROM THE
CAREFULLY-PLACED NAME
BUT FROM THE DESIGN
VALUES OF THE PRODUCT

Clearing the way

CLIENT	
	Hong Kong Government
	Hong Kong
DESIGNERS	
	Alan Chan & Springpoint
	Hong Kong *London, UK.*
PRODUCT / SERVICE	
	Hong Kong International
	Airport Core programme

the **background**

The full opening of the new Hong Kong Airport, scheduled for late 1998, will mark the conclusion of the largest transport infrastructure project in the world. Not just the creation of an airport able to handle 87 million passengers and 9 million tonnes of freight annually, but a bridge 300 foot longer than the Golden Gate bridge in San Francisco, a new motorway and rail service, and a new city for 200,000 people. All this is being built on a group of islands in Hong Kong Bay (yes, it's the world's largest land reclamation project as well).

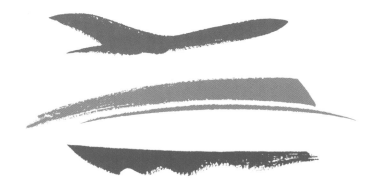

香 港 機 場 核 心 計 劃
HONG KONG AIRPORT
CORE PROGRAMME

the brief

The construction of the new Hong Kong airport affected the lives of tens of thousands of people in the city. The brief for a project logo was aimed at facilitating communication between the team building the airport and the communities, business interests and political authorities involved or touched by the

the research

This very high profile undertaking had to be explained to a large number of constituencies; firstly to the people of Hong Kong itself, whose daily lives would be affected by three or four years of construction work, secondly to the political, business and financial communities in Hong Kong and China, and thirdly to a wide range of international business interests, for whom Hong Kong is seen as a central feature in the business landscape of South East Asia. This task needs communication skills, and so the Hong Kong Government approached Alan Chan, a designer based in Hong Hong, and the London-based consultancy Springpoint to advise them on getting 'the right message to the right people.' It rapidly became clear that the scale of the project made it of central importance not only to Hong Kong and China but also to the whole Pacific area, indeed even to the world. One key concept was Interlink, which referred not only to the chain Islands where the airport and the new city were to be built, but also to the transport links between site and existing city, and thirdly, and more importantly, how this new link to and from Hong Kong would impact on the whole region.

Further verbal concepts were developed using 'brainstorming' sessions of Cantonese, Manadarin and English speakers (as any names found had to be acceptable in all three languages). Some idea of the scale of the programme can be judged by the fact that these sessions were only to produce a first list of one thousand possibilities. This multi-lingual approach was necessary in view of the range of different constituencies and agencies with whom the design had to communicate.

At the same time a number of graphic ideas were studied, towards developing a visual approach to graphic communication. These visual studies included abstract images, as well as forms based on the rich tradition of Chinese imagery, in which, for example, the dragon symbolises strength and goodness, and the phoenix is associated with peace, prosperity and plenty.

SOME OF THE GRAPHIC
SYMBOLS DEVISED WHILE
CREATING THE IDENTITY

the solution

The final design was created by Mark Pierce of Springpoint. It can be read on a number of levels. Firstly as an image of a plane in flight. Secondly as representations of air, land, and water. Thirdly, through its calligraphic style, as both classical and contemporary and Chinese. And fourthly, it recalls the Chinese ideogram for three, representing the trinity of land, sea and air, or travel in all three media.

'More than just a symbol, the new identity adds up to an unmistakable and unique visual language' Fiona Gilmore

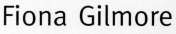

the assessment

The design, with its fine nuances of meaning, is deceptively simple, because it is in fact the result of a complex process of consultation and review, which in turn often created new challenges and interests independent of the main aims of the process. In 'telling the world about the world's largest infrastructure project, as Fiona Gilmore of Springpoint describes the task, design has been used as an agent for managing change. 'The logo, she explains, 'is a key element in our targeting strategy, part of a language that would be instantly recognisable and, at the same time, flexible enough to talk to people as different as children and international businessmen, using different phrases from the same visual vocabulary.'

Treading the Measure

CLIENT
Ballet-Tech
New York, USA

DESIGNERS
Pentagram
New York, USA

PRODUCT / SERVICE
Dance company

the background

Cultural organisations in the dance and theatre world have a public image and reputation which is in part a general one and in part based upon the renown of individual pieces or events. (Actors, it is said – rather unfairly – 'are only as good as their last performances.') So building an ongoing identity for such an organisation requires both firmness and flexibility, particularly where the organisation, as here, contains three individual elements that have a special relationship with each other.

In 1996 the dance impresario Eliot Feld decided to reorganise and rename his various ballet activities: previously there had been an adult troupe, which performed regularly at New York's Joyce Theater, called Feld Ballets/NY, a children's troupe, Kids Dance, and a school offering free tuition, P.S. Ballet. These were to come under the new name, Ballet Tech, and Feld approached 'Paula Scher at' Pentagram in New York to create a visual identity for the new organisation, under which the individual components would retain their individuality but benefit from the attention that could be refocused on the organisation as a whole.

Ballet Tech begins by auditioning third and forth grade schoolchildren, and offers them a ballet opportunity right through to membership of a professional company.

BALLET·TECH

THE COMPANY

KIDS DANCE

NYC PUBLIC SCHOOL
FOR DANCE

the brief

The task here was to develop a logo and associated imagery for publicity and promotion for a dance
company strongly involved in educational work. The combination of photography and type is particularly

the solution

The new name was chosen to balance the elegance and precision of traditional ballet and the contemporary artistry that is the hallmark of Feld's choreography. Centring around a high-energy, innovative approach to dance, the identity had to link and identify the different elements. The adult troupe was renamed The Ballet-Tech Company, and the P.S. School the NYC Public School for Dance, while Kids Dance retained the original name. The new name also linked the structure of the component elements. Each year, as they have for the last two decades, Ballet Tech offers free ballet auditions to some 35,000 children in New York City schools, and from these about 1,000 are offered free tuition at ballet classes. By sixth grade, the most talented of these children are studying dance every day at the school, as well as completing their academic program. The Kids Dance company is drawn from children at the school, while the Ballet Tech company is now comprised entirely of dancers who have graduated from the school. Ballet Tech is thus a unique organisation, with a continuous development programme and internal links within its elements. It is not surprising that the different elements, and particularly the Kids Dance events, have become firm favourites on the New York ballet circuit.

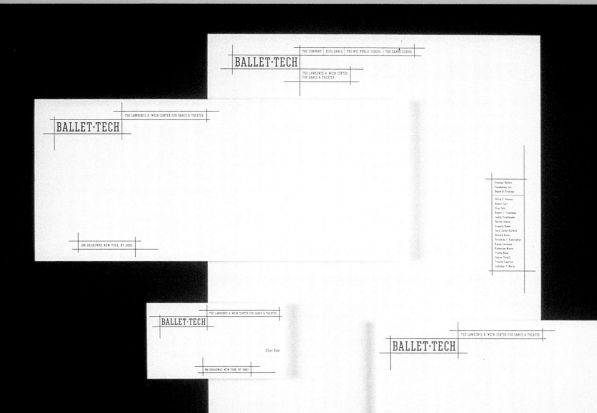

the development

The identity comprises three related elements: typography, 'scaffolding' and photography. The type selected is a condensed Egyptian serif, used in capitals for the element names. This is printed in a deep Prussian blue where colour is used. The photographic element uses photos by Lois Greenfield of individuals or pairs of dancers as cut-out figures. These are printed as monochromes overlaid with graduated colour tones. The typographic scaffolding – designer Paula Scher's term - uses a framework of heavy rules to both isolate and link the different elements. The presentation launch logo uses the name Ballet Tech on an offset colour ground as the central element with the company names above and to the right and the strapline 'a new company from Eliot Feld' below. The main logo uses a different colour scheme (red scaffolding for blue, with the name reversed out of a blue block) and the three element names listed below. The Kids Dance logo uses red scaffolding, a blue name out of yellow and the Ballet Tech name, smaller, above in blue. These typographical elements can be laid over or around the photographic images.

The combination of typographic scaffolding and graduated photographs of dancers creates the Ballet Tech look.

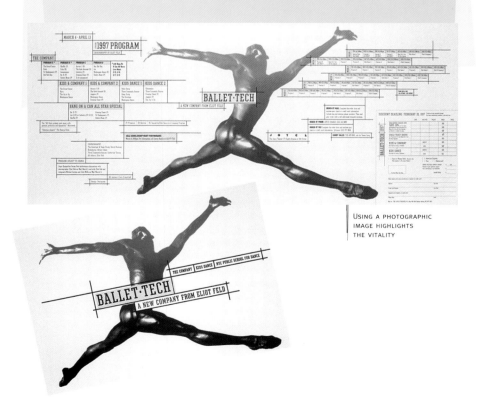

USING A PHOTOGRAPHIC
IMAGE HIGHLIGHTS
THE VITALITY

BALLET·TECH

KIDS DANCE

SEASON BEGINS AUGUST 20TH

Program A

The Grand Canon.
Ogive. Chi.
Ludwig Gambits

Program B

Harbinger. Clave.
With Dew Upon
Their Feet.
The Jig Is Up.

	MON	TUES	WED	THURS	FRI	SAT MAT	SAT EVE
	8/7 A opens	8/8 A	8/9 B opens	8/10 B	8/11 A	8/12 B	8/12 A
	8/14 B	8/15 B	8/16 A	8/17 A	8/18 B	8/19 A	8/19 B

FOR TICKETS CALL JOYCECHARGE 212-242-0800

For Program Information Only, Call 212-777-7710

JOYCE

The Joyce Theater 175 Eighth Avenue at 19th. St.

VISUAL PROMOTION IS
ESSENTIAL FOR BOTH
THE KIDS DANCE
PROJECT AND
BALLET TECH...

MARCH 4 - APRIL 13

BALLET·TECH KIDS DAN

the assessment

The result has a distinctive visual feel, but within that it has flexibility while offering the chance to exploit the opportunities and requirements of different formats, whether they be letterheads, programmes, invitations, poster campaigns, press advertising, T-shirts and even advertisements on buses. This visual language leads to the creation of a Ballet-Tech look, a consistent but varied approach that ballet enthusiasts will come to recognise and endorse. As the programme of dance events and the membership of the different companies will change over time, so-unlike the case for a corporation, the logo needs room to evolve and develop to meet new needs and opportunities, for example in incorporating images of dancers from new productions.

Achieving such variety while maintaining consistency requires both a high level of visual imagination and a clear understanding of the potential and risks of such a solution from the outset. Too tight a structure could rapidly become ossified and so dated, while too free an arrangement would fail to build the links between the different companies and the schools and lose the chance to create a firm identity for this very special cultural institution in the public mind.

...WHETHER IN NEWSPAPER ADS OR ON BUSES.

Design from disaster

CLIENT

Düsseldorf Airport
Berlin, Germany

DESIGNERS

MetaDesign
Berlin, Germany

PRODUCT / SERVICE

Airport signage and identity

the background

At Düsseldorf airport, a fire in the main terminal building killed eighteen people in April 1996. The event, Germany's worst civilian airport disaster, sent shock-waves through the German airport system, in which most airports are run by public bodies or municipalities. After the fire the airport was being run from temporary buildings and tents, and the passenger traffic of 20,000 per day was set to rise to 70,000 when the holiday period began six weeks later, as Düsseldorf is the home airport for LTU, Germany's largest charter company. The business of an airport consists, largely, in moving people on foot from landside to airside, a process in which signage is essential for efficiency, and, even more importantly in the context, for safety. The loss of the main terminal building had left the existing signage system in collapse.

But it was not until the beginning of June that the Berlin-based designers MetaDesign were called in to advise on the signage problem. 'We realised that the deadline was very tight,' Bruno Schmidt of MetaDesign explains, 'so we accepted the brief on condition that the airport management made two people available full time with the authority to take decisions, twenty-four hours a day, everyday. This they accepted.' It was not the first hard choice the management had to make. 'German airports are run by rather formal, stiff companies,' says Schmidt, 'and Düsseldorf was in shock after the fire. They began to realise that change was going to be necessary – a more competitive attitude, for example, with the threat from Frankfurt and Amsterdam airports not so far away' and to achieve this, a new identity, not just a wayfinding system, would be needed. The project, based on MetaDesign's analysis, became within the same time-frame, not only the new signage system, but the creation of a new identity for the airport, for which the signage system would be the first element.

When a fire destroyed the terminal at Düsseldorf Airport, there was an immediate need for new signage so that the airport could continue to function. This provided a starting point for the creation of a new

SIGNAGE POINTED
THE WAY TO THE
CREATION OF A
NEW IDENTITY

the solution

Within the six weeks MetaDesign produced a new signage programme, using a new typeface, researched to have a high degree of legibility. It also used a key colour of green under white type. 'Our research showed that most German airports had new buildings with new identities, as buildings from the 1950s had been replaced, for example at Munich and Stuttgart. We were going to have a new building, so a new signage system was needed. In selecting the typeface, legibility was the key quality we sought. As to the colour system, MetaDesign decided to abandon the previous black and yellow system, and divide a system that would also distinguish between service signage and signs specifically for arriving or departing passengers. Some colour choices were already in use as part of the identities of other airports. As to the colour, some choices were already in use by other airports – Frankfurt uses white and royal blue, Munich pale blue, Stuttgart grey. 'The green also forms a link to the colours of the local Land,' says Schmidt, 'and it forms the starting point for the development of the identity for the rebuilt airport.' The 2,500 new signs were in place in time for the holiday period, thanks to using local contractors. 'We deliberately mounted most of the signs on provisional systems such as scaffolding. This was partly because signage position would change as the buildings were rebuilt, but also to fit in with the building work going on around.' MetaDesign also developed a code for sign positioning on the master plan, so that the future development of the sign system and implementation of new signs and the identity could be handled by the airport in a flexible but correct way.

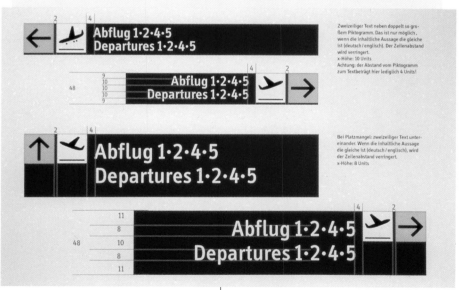

the solution

Airport signage is a mute witness to the changes taking place in the organisation, functioning and culture of airports. Successful signage programmes do not merely speed the travellers on their way, they contribute also to the total genius loci: they need to be planned to live alongside the airport's own identity, and amid the welter of other liveries, from airline colours to the retail element that is making increasing claims for attention in airport space. So the task of designing successful integrated systems becomes harder, more challenging. And airports are waking up to the need to get signage and identity right in a different commercial world. As Bruno Schmidt wryly observes, 'profit does create change.'

COLOUR CODING FOR DIFFERENT
KINDS OF INFORMATION MAKES
COMMUNICATION CLEARER

Vintage enjoyment

C L I E N T
Vinopolis/Wineworld
London, UK.

D E S I G N E R S
Lewis Moberly
London, UK.

P R O D U C T / S E R V I C E
Wine vaults

the background

Feast on wine, or fast on water,
And your honour shall stand sure
God Almighty's son and daughter,
He the valiant, she the pure

If an angel out of heaven
Brings you other things to drink
Thank him for his kind intentions
Go and pour them down the sink.

So wrote the English poet G.K. Chesterton in the early years of this century in an entertaining moral fable that went on to castigate cocoa ('a cad and coward') and other drinks. The poem does not mention beer, though elsewhere beer is, in Chesterton's view, the quintessential Englishman's drink, while wine is for the French, Italians and Spaniards. Beer remained the staple alcohol of England for a long time, but recently wine drinking has become increasingly popular, partly as a result of more Britons travelling abroad, as a result of successful wine promotions in supermarkets, and as a result of a 'café culture' breaking into the dated world of the English pub.

The Vinopolis venture is a consequence of this new market for wine. Built on the south bank of the Thames in London, near the Globe Theatre, it will, when it opens in November 1998, offer an experience of wines from around the world and of the history of wine in the first visitor attraction of its kind in Britain. Housed in immense old wine vaults, Vinopolis (the City of Wine) has a suite of presentation rooms (designed by Jasper Jacob, with architects Hunter and Partners), together with a tasting hall and several multicultural restaurants. Whether such a new way of experiencing wine will succeed is, at the time of writing, too early to tell.

VINOPOLIS
CITY OF WINE

A new approach to the enjoyment and selling of wine, through a tourist attraction, calls for an identity that is cheerful, relaxed and immediate. The initial logo also serves as a development point for signage and packaging, so maintaining a consistency of offer across the whole activity of the new enterprise.

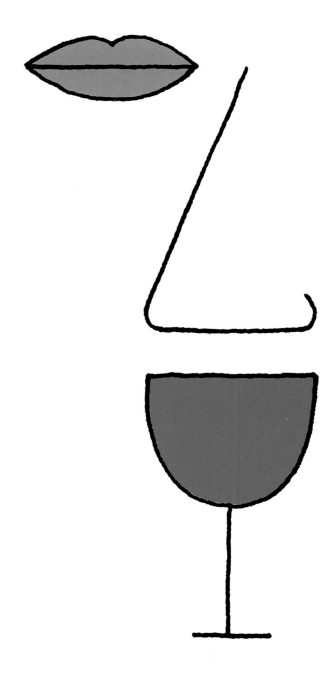

the solution

For the corporate identity the parent company, Wineworld, commissioned the London-based consultants Lewis Moberly. The brief was for a logo, stationery designs, carrier bags and wine labels for wine sales, and signage for the area. The designers' approach was based on the sensual aspects of wine: colour, bouquet and taste - the traditional tools of the winetaster. The result is a simple and very subtle logo, slightly abstract. It can be read as a vertical pattern, like samurai's flag: mouth, nose, wine glass. Or it can be read as a face: blue eye, profile nose, red mouth. Is the blue shape a mouth or an eye? Is the red shape a mouth or a glass?

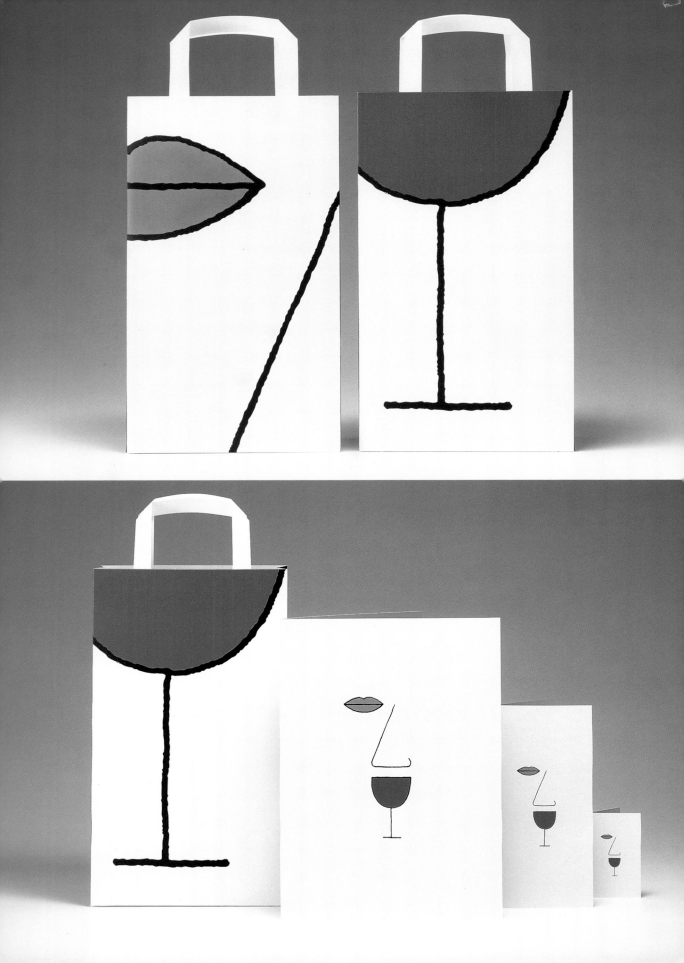

the assessment

These elements are hand drawn for the logo, and accompanied by the Vinopolis name in a classical serif face, with City of Wine beneath in sans serif. On the carrier bags elements from the design are carried over in detail, with the Vinopolis name vertically in the fold. According to design director Mary Lewis of Lewis Moberly, 'the identity simply sums up the sensual pleasure of wine. The logo is abstracted throughout, reflecting the infinite variants of the subject. Wine is now very much part of British life: we've moved on from being a beer-swilling nation.' Would Chesterton have agreed, or approved?

what

A brand is the visual identity of a related group of products or services from a common source.

A brand is related to the marketplace (or often a specific market) rather than the general economic activity of the company.

A brand consists of the logos, colours, names, pack shapes or slogans unique to it.

A brand may or may not contain elements derived from the corporate identity of the parent company.

is a brand ?

A brand is one of the most important design equities owned by a company. The Coca-Cola bottle is one of the most widely recognised objects in the world, though, curiously, the name of its designer is unknown. (Raymond Loewy, with his usual enthusiasm, claimed to have designed it, but in fact all his office did was modify the original shape for use in vending machines). The name Coca-Cola is also one of the most widely recognised names in the world as well. How has this been achieved? The central realisation that has brought this about is, in my view, understanding that the brand is not merely the label of a product, but can also, through association, be the foundation of a lifestyle. That is to say, the product can embody aspirations and values that users of the product identify with, so in using the product they feel part of a group of like-minded people. Not only does such a successful product have a personality of its own, it expresses a way of living, a set of values, an affirmation of choices. Coca-Cola has built this personality through advertising campaigns and promotions that position the drink clearly in a relaxed, happy, youthful environment, essentially participatory and informal. Such a lifestyle is linked to a certain vision of America (another major brand, Marlboro cigarettes, uses a different vision of America in a similar way as the bedrock of its success). And having created this environment for the product, the satisfaction the product delivers must match those expectations. Achieving this kind of success requires consistency of a high order, and above all focus. Focus in the sense of continually analysing and researching the qualities and values of the product and its environment, and its mythic image. Not only does the product itself have to be absolutely right all the time, it must show an understanding of the evolving and changing environment in which it operates. This is a high risk strategy, in some ways, because if you fall from the top you go all the way down, and because diversification also becomes extremely difficult: you have to create an independent and different personality for any alternative products, since feeding them of the main one risks diluting its unique quality.

OXO

BIRDS EYE

FLEUR/CAMARADE

Starring Starck

CLIENT
OAO
Lima, Brussels, Belgium

DESIGNERS
Studio Starck
Issy les Moulineaux, Franc

PRODUCT / SERVICE
Organic and
vegetarian foods

the background

Philippe Starck is one of the most famous product and interior designers in the world. His hotel interiors at the Royalton in New York and the Mondrian in Los Angeles and elsewhere, his chairs for Kartell in Italy and XO in France, his consumer goods for Thomson and his kitchenware for Alessi, including the famous Juicy Salif lemon squeezer, have made him into a design hero. He is also now a vegetarian, and with his usual enthusiasm in autumn 1998 launched himself into the world of vegetarian and organic foods. Together with the Belgian company Lima, one of the oldest and best-known producers of vegetarian products, he has created a new brand, OAO.

Starck finds that conventional attitudes to vegetarian food sometimes spring from a form of social denial, or a misplaced altruism, or a conservative, backward-looking view. He doesn't share any of these. Rather he believes that killing to eat is, put simply, bestial and out-of-date. If human society is to evolve into a caring and loving society, then that is an inherited trait it has to lose. But looking at the available products and their presentation, he felt his future vision was an option that had been overlooked. It was, structurally, a marginal business, only selling to those already convinced of the vegetarian argument. What if he could recruit a new market, among younger people, who are concerned about their health, about the food industry, about the treatment of animals, but who do not share the whole of the rest of the vegetarian ethos?

The launch of a new range of organic and vegetarian foods, created by the leading designer Philippe Starck, uses an invented name and an approach to packaging that lets the customer understand immediately what is on offer. The challenge for the designer was to balance the presence of the identity

the development

The OAO range is the result of this initiative, containing over forty products, including olive oil and vinegar, salt, pepper and gomasio condiment, organic spaghetti, couscous, noodles and two types of rice. Together with biscuits, rice cakes, nuts, pasta sauces, muesli, cornflakes and oat milk, three different pâte's and two sets of instant snacks from the Biolino range by Lima, one a four-pack of breakfast mixes, the other a six-pack of lunch or evening dishes, there is also – most importantly – organic champagne and wine. Because the collection is not about denial, but about inclusion, about celebration not isolation.

Patrick Grandqvist, who worked with Starck on developing the branding and packaging, explains the brand concept in terms of honesty and clarity. 'Our starting point was that the customer should see exactly what is in the packet, and that the packet should contain the maximum amount of information on the organic origins and nutritional qualities of the contents.' At the same time the packaging has to have a completely contemporary look, to set it apart from other products in the field.

'Saying "you can",
not "you must":
the difference
between a
contemporary
approach which
values the

individual to a
conservative or
ideological
approach which
denies the
individual.'
Philippe Starck

the development

This is achieved by a basic white look, with information panels overprinted on grey or yellow. The OAO logo, in letter spaced sans serif capitals, is printed in grey. The name OAO is an invented name, based on the Japanese word for peace, oa, not an acronym (although it could stand for Organic Agricultural Original) because the products initially sell across three languages, French, Flemish and English. The packaging materials, as a matter of principle, are recycled and biodegradable, and the choice of packaging solutions is deliberately innovative, establishing OAO as a lifestyle brand not just a health one. So the oat milk is in a familiar Tetrapak carton but with embossed lettering (the first time this has been achieved on Tetrapak) and the instant snacks are in holders which transform into bowls: you don't have to transfer the contents to another container.

ORGANIC WHEAT SYRUP

PRODUCT VISIBILITY IS
A KEY ELEMENT IN THE
TOTAL OFFER

the **assessment**

OAO represents Starck's first personal venture into branding, though he has been involved with packaging design for his products from Alessi and for electronic consumer goods as art director for Thomson. His interest in the project is as much political as personal, for he sees designers as under a social obligation to help create a fairer, less consuming, less isolated society. His view is that humanity is a species in mutation, and that designers can be the agents of evolutionary change in this process. The OAO range is one of several steps he is taking towards turning his ideas into action.

The OAO branding expertly combines a relaxed, modern lifestyle look, so reaching a new market for the products, with the obligation to honesty and openness that is innate in the underlying ethos of organic and vegetarian food. It avoids the clichés of naturalness which can so easily slip into thoughtless eco-fervour, or the parallel positioning adopted by other products in the field that suggest the customer is getting meat-free meat. OAO marks a new start, not only for Starck, but for the merchandising and branding of organic products.

Food colouring

CLIENT
Bird's Eye Foods
Walton-on-Thames, UK.

DESIGNERS
Springpoint
London, UK.

PRODUCT/SERVICE
Frozen foods

the background

Birds Eye frozen foods are part of the Unilever group (they are marketed elsewhere in the world under different names such as Iglo). The main brand is well established, with its blue and white logo well known from packaging and from television and press advertising. The brand equity includes solid values of quality, nutrition, freshness, and convenience. - these terms were identified by the client as keys to its marketing and presentation strategy, and packaging designs for all brands are evaluated according to these criteria.

The task for the designers was to develop a purely visual language that would relate families of products under the main name. The solution is based on relating colours to taste sensations, and is a

the research

Mark Pearce of Springpoint has been the designer responsible for the brand's recent development. 'Birds Eye had a number of sub-brands for different product areas such as meats and vegetables, each identified by group names,' he explains, 'but market research showed these sub-brands were not identified by consumers, either on their own or, what was worse, as part of the main Bird's Eye brand.' In other words, the sub-brands were not working.

'What we set out to do was to lose the sub-brand names, which were a distraction, and instead concentrate on the main name, building a "Birds Eye world" within which there would be a range of individual offers sharing the values of the main brand but making their own statements.' This was not to be done by naming, but by visual clues linked to sensory aspects of the foods themselves: the sizzle of grilled meat, the aroma of cooked chicken, the crunch of fresh vegetables. Food is a total sensory experience, involving sight, taste and smell, with different foods evoking different perceptions (for example research showed that chicken had different consumer perceptions from red meats, as did potatoes from other vegetables). Springpoint wanted the branding to reflect this variety and totality.

'Design is a visual language'
Mark Pearce

THE PACK REDESIGNS SHOW HOW
VISUAL RATHER THAN BRAND
CODING IS MORE EFFECTIVE

the **solution**

To achieve this, Springpoint created a visual map within which each of these food offers could be located, and thus linked back visually to the main logo, a system of distinctness plus proximity which can be added to as new products enter to the range.

IN THE CASE OF CHICKEN
THE SIZZLE PART OF THE
COLOUR MAP IS USED ON
THE PACK

the assessment

Letting products develop their own visual language is also a key area in brand development.

'Design is a visual language', Pearce insists. His skill in creating a visual metaphor for the complexities of offers and equities within the Birds Eye range is a tribute to his ability as a visual linguist, and a reminder that design success does not depend on argument but appearance (and that durable appearance has to be well argued)!

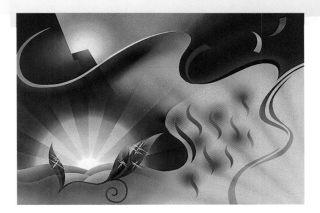

Finding friends

CLIENT

Worlds Brands
London, UK.

DESIGNERS

Grey Matter
London, UK.

PRODUCT / SERVICE

Cognac gift packs

the background

Fleur and Camarade are niche marketing in niche markets. Grey Matter is an established London consultancy for logo and product design (in the old terminology: they call themselves brand and product developers), working with a small group of long-term clients, including Worlds Brands, who specialise in gift products for the international duty-free market. Grey Matter recently won a Design Effectiveness Award for Fleur, a bottle of cognac for Worlds Brands. This product, for sale in duty free shops only, is targeted at young Asian women travellers. The complete logo and branding package for Fleur was directly aimed at this narrow group.

the brief

The client was looking for ways of bringing cognac to the attention of highly specific Asian markets, starting with a women-only market with Fleur and then for males with Camarade. The packaging plus identity solution not only created successful products, but through point of sale material gave them a

the solution

A Russian doll of niche marketing, perhaps, but one only achieved through a close understanding of the client's approach and market. This holistic approach to design runs through an open office structure of 'thinking creatives and creative thinkers' and into client relations seen as teamwork not hierarchy. 'Asking a client why is always a challenge, but a necessary one for a true relationship,' Sean O'Flynn of Grey Matter points out. 'The client realised that cognac was not being bought by this part of the market, because the product was branded and presented in an inappropriate way.' So in creating the brand image of the product, Grey Matter deliberately used visual links to luxury goods with which the intended customers were familiar, especially perfumery and sports products. And in pursuit of their view of not being compartmented, but 'compartmented plus', Fleur is not a stand alone product but part of a future Haute Couture brand.

the development

Fleur has been joined on the same duty free shelves by Camarade, a similar cognac for male travellers. Both products break the old rules of branding, since neither use the conventional visual language of alcohol branding. Fleur looks as if it might be a perfume or cosmetic product, with its pale cream box and floral graphics, and Camarade could be a sports or personal hygiene kit, in a green cloth and rubber container decorated with dog-tag fasteners. But both products have been very well received in their particular markets.

'We weren't trying to create a brand image that matched our expectations,' Stuart Serjent of Grey Matter explains, 'but the expectations of the target market. We looked at what young Asian travellers expected of cognac, and what they knew about it. At the top end of the market there were well-established famous names, closely linked with the culture of gifts. Below that there were less expensive brands that were purchased by experienced cognac drinkers. We were not competing with either of these. We were making an alternative offer, suggesting a personal purchase to clients unfamiliar with cognac but curious about it. To achieve this we had to put the product, through its branding, into the context of personal purchases, not gifts purchases.' So the metaphor the two brands use are perfumes and cosmetics for women, and sports goods for men. The metaphorical envelope reassures the customer that he or she is not buying something too unfamiliar.

What Grey Matter achieved was to create logos that had their own lifestyle. 'For the target market Camarade had to have a Western, contemporary feel, even if it also plugs into Asian notions,' Stuart Serjent of Grey Matter explains. 'Our aim was to create a world in which the product lives, with which the customers could identify, feel one-to-one with the myths and signals generated by the product. Camarade presents cognac as a social drink, to be shared with friends. The bag is a travel accessory, as well as a giftwrap.' The point of sale material for the bag is a series of images of a group of young men having fun together: a bit naughty, but basically in line. Grey Matter's success with the designs for both Fleur and Camarade came from their taking a wider view, and letting the brief and its market prevail over the established concepts of how to brand products in a particular field.

'Asking a client "why" is always a challenge, but a necessary one for a true relationship'
Sean O'Flynn

what is

corporate culture
and brand culture?

orporate culture is the expression of a corporate
hilosophy in terms of the company's relations with
thers internally and externally. The corporate
hilosophy is often set out as a 'mission statement'
r 'code of practice.'

Corporate culture is not only expressed through the
internal workings or commercial activity of the
company: it also has an important role in external
relations, for example in the fields of generic
advertising and sponsorship.

Corporate culture links the mission statements, codes
of practice, marketing and development methods and
corporate identity into a continuous and evolving
whole. For this reason the development of a new
corporate identity or the development of a revised
one can often be linked to a restatement or
repositioning of a corporate philosophy.

Brand culture is the same concept applied to the
development and management of a brand. Brand
culture may be directed more specifically at the
marketplace (while corporate culture will need to take
into account the company's relations with
governmental agencies, international and national
regulatory bodies, and the whole spectrum of public
opinion).

Brand culture cannot diverge too far from the corporate culture of the parent
without risking its own credibility. The degree of divergence possible depends
on the perceived relation between parent and brand. Some parents are very
close to their brands – Coca-Cola, for example, Kodak or Microsoft. Others are
more distant – a company such as Nestlé, for example, has an own-name brand
as well as a range of semi-independent brands of considerable importance.
Some companies appear to operate brands at arms length: in Europe, for
example, General Motors owns a number of car marquees including Opel and
Vauxhall, but keeps well in the background in terms of market presence
(whatever degree of actual control they may operate over their subsidiaries.)
The success of a brand or corporate culture can be seen in the degree of
identification between company and consumer, the extent to which the outside
world trusts the company, or believes in the world' its products inhabit. This
relationship is a continuously changing one, which brand and identity
managers need to monitor and nurture constantly. The fact that the success in
question can never be exactly quantified does not mean that its existence is
not essential to a company's prosperity. Some years ago Nike, the makers of
sports shoes, goods and clothes, opened Nike World in New York. Unlike the
Disney and Warner shops that are now found in many capitals, Nike World was
not a retailing venture. It was a physical celebration of the sports-based culture
that Nike has created around its products. As such, the shop displayed Nike
products, showed videos of sports stars sponsored by Nike, and contained Nike
advertising and promotional material, as well as games and events. Nike has
used sponsorship and advertising to position its products as the equivalence
of excellence. In so doing they it has moved the sports shoe through fashion
accessory into lifestyle necessity, while still retaining its integrity as a product
for use in sport at the most demanding competitive levels. This twin track
approach – excellent technology combined with desirability – is what underlies
Nike's success. Motor manufacturers use a similar strategy in sponsoring motor
racing, but with the drawback that the distance between the products – the
Formula One car and the family sports saloon – is too wide. Not so for Nike,
who have developed their position to the extent that even their tickmark logo
on its own conveys the excitement and assurance of the brand.

THE SAVOY

LAWYERS COMMITTEE
FOR HUMAN RIGHTS

OXYGEN/ATOMIC SKI

TECHNIQUEST

CEARNS & BROWN

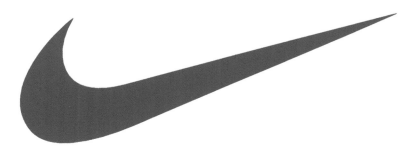

NIKE'S SUCCESS AS A BRAND
MEANS THAT THE TICK MARK
ALONE STANDS FOR SPORTS
EXCELLENCE

Invisible assets

CLIENT

Direct Line
Croydon, UK

DESIGNERS

Northcross
Edinburgh, Scotland

PRODUCT/SERVICE

Insurance and financial services

the background

The reality of stone, bricks and mortar were the traditional visual vocabulary of banks and insurance houses. Marble halls with columnated porticos sprang up around the nineteenth-century world, physical symbols of the solidity, prestige and reputation of banking. Necessary symbols, because the increasing regulation of the banking industry, and the conformity of services they offered, meant there was little to choose between different bankers in terms of product or services.

The deregulation of banking and the development of credit cards and ATMs (automated teller machines) began to change that. When Citibank introduced automatic banking in New York in the mid-1980s, it went to great lengths to appear user-friendly and reassure customers that a human banker would always be available. Surveys, however, rapidly showed that customers in fact preferred dealing with the machines! A decade later the human-machine mix of banking has got considerably more sophisticated. ATMs are now situated where people spend money – in supermarkets, malls and airports – not just in the walls of banks. And within the bank building, the grills and armoured glass separating the customers from the money (and the staff) have been moved back, to create table space for meeting your personal banker. This change in space has been in response to a change in ethos.

Insurance and financial services are invisible products, doubly so when sold by telephone. The designer's task was to develop a personality for the company, through its logo and through a series of promotions and publications that would make the public feel in touch with the company.

As well as
defining identity
guidelines the
designers also
created a
customer
magazine,
The Answer

SPONSORSHIP IS PART OF DEVELOPING THE BRAND, AS HERE AT THE EASTBOURNE LADIES TENNIS TOURNAMENT, FOR WHICH A HOUSE-SIZED VERSION OF THE LOGO WAS CREATED

the solution

If the bank without a bank clerk, why not a bank without a building? That was the idea behind Direct Line, a telephone-based subsidiary of the Midland Bank offering initially motoring insurance and 'later' services such as mortgages and pensions. Direct Line's logo – a jaunty red telephone on wheels – began as an advertising image. It has been largely developed since by Edinburgh consultancy Northcross. They have created a series of exhibitions, a customer magazine, and various promotional offers. John Slater of Northcross explains "the marketing position of Direct Line was the people's champion". We had to create a personality around this.' This involved two major projects: the first was building a house-sized telephone as an exhibition stand, not only for indoor use at events such as the Ideal Home Exhibition, but also out of doors as a support to Direct Line's sponsorship of the Ladies' Tennis Championship in Eastbourne each year. 'Building a house in the shape of a phone is difficult enough: building one that can be taken down and put up again is another matter,' Slater comments. The second concept was Phoneham, a model town where the vehicles are red telephones. 'We wanted to entertain the customer, to put some spark and adventure into the insurance business.' Northcross's approach has been to take the bravura of the concept at its face value, and run with it.

DIRECT LINE'S TENNI
SPONSORSHIP REACHES
WIDER MARKET THROUG
THE VIRTUAL TENNI
EVENT PRESENTED A
TRADE FAIR

virtual
TENNIS

THE PHONEHOUSE LARGE SCALE
MODEL IS SHOWN AT TRADE
EXHIBITIONS, WHILE PHONEHAM
IS A PERMANENT MODEL SITE

NIKE'S SUCCESS AS A BRAND
MEANS THAT THE TICK MARK
ALONE STANDS FOR SPORTS
EXCELLENCE

Walking the dog

CLIENT

Klöckner & Co.
Duisberg, Germany

DESIGNERS

Wolff Olins
London, UK.

PRODUCT/SERVICE

Steel stockholders and suppliers

the background

Steel stockholders buy steel elements from mills and other producers, and sell on to construction companies and manufacturers. It is a specialised, inter-professional commodity business, where success depends on selecting likely product lines, anticipating price and supply fluctuations, and understanding the demand cycles of the different user markets. Klöckner was well established in the German market when it became part of the larger Weber industrial group in the 1980s, and from this new position the company proceeded to make a number of acquisitions in Europe (in Germany itself, France, Spain, Holland and Britain) and in the USA, a reflection of an increasingly international market for steel that was replacing national systems of supply.

klöckner & co

multi metal distribution

the brief

The challenge was to reposition a steel products group that had grown from national to international scope in a highly specialised market, and so create synergy and a common purpose between the different companies in the group. The dog motif devised for this becomes an excellent metaphor for the internal restructuring and new vision sought by the client.

the **research**

While this expansion made good business sense, the identity of Klöckner itself risked being diluted (in a business where an established name was a major advantage), not only within Weber but more widely, as there were a number of other companies called by the same or similar names in the field. In the mid-1990s the company asked the London-based agency Wolff Olins for their help. The brief also asked them to look at ways of creating more synergy between the different companies in the group, while leaving them autonomy in their own markets.

As Lee Coomber of Wolff Olins explains, 'Klöckner is operating in a closed, professional market, so the emphasis was on using any new design as an agent for internal change rather than for external perceptions.' So, for example, inventing a new name for the group would have been a retrograde step, and a waste of existing goodwill. Instead Wolff Olins devised a strategy of repositioning. 'We put it to them that they were not in the business of shifting steel, but satisfying their customer's. Coomber explains or that they were in a service rather than a manufacturing business.' This strategic shift would allow top management to redirect the activities of the group in a more coherent way, with the implementation of the new identity as the start of this process.

The board of directors of Klöckner devised a new mission statement, with Wolff Olin's help. This consisted of a statement of vision and of principles. The vision: to become the worldwide leader in steel and metal distribution. The principles were fourfold:
— Market leadership is our goal.
— Adding value is our competitive advantage.
— Improving our performance is our task.
— We are open, creative and consequent.

THE RUNNING DOG SYMBOL
ADDS A LIGHTER TOUCH TO
SPONSORSHIP PROJECTS AND
INTER-COMPANY MAILINGS

Our new identity is a symbol for all that is best in customer service

Like a dog, we are both servant and friend. We fetch and carry, responding to our customers' needs with enthusiasm and energy.

bigger **faster better**

We are reliable and loyal, fulfilling our promises and treating our customers fairly. And we are always on the move, ready to deliver goods quickly and efficiently.

You will see our dog in all sorts of places – on everything from letters, signs and trucks, to football shirts and hot-air balloons.

Our symbol reflects our shared commitment to our future. We aim to make it a hallmark of distribution excellence.

the **solution**

With this to guide them, Wolff Olins started looking for a visual metaphor for the group's activities, and for a corporate style. The ideas of service, fidelity and promptness suggested the notion of a dog retrieving a ball, and this is what Wolff Olins worked on as a visual cue. 'It had to be a simple outline, like a cartoon image,' Coomber explains, 'because it had to be light, a little naïve, and slightly whimsical at the same time. We tried lots of different images, but the version we finally chose was almost the very first sketch that we had done.' The dog, in the corporate blue with a red ball in its mouth, is used only in one pose in the finished identity, though in the presentational booklet of vision and principles it appears in a number of poses, while the red ball was used as a theme-motif in the corporate video to launch the new identity. The blue and red, together with a standard typeface, Bliss, is also set up as standard for all corporate letterheads, visiting cards, publications and signage. The red is reserved for the group name (which is always set in lowercase, and accompanied by the strapline 'multi-metal distribution'). The dog image is used sparingly, and with special attention to scale: small on stationery or business cards, large on the sides of trucks or warehouse walls, with hardly any intermediate applications. The intention is that all staff, throughout the group, will become familiar with the image and the relationship of element to group, as will customers. 'Over time,' the design guidelines handbook explains to the group companies, 'you will become recognised through our dog as much as you are known by your own name.'

THE DOG ACTS AS A RUNNING
MOTIF THROUGH THE BOOKLET
EXPLAINING THE COMPANY'S
NEW MISSION STATEMENT

Name
Function/Department

Direct line
Direct fax

Date

ASD plc
Valley Farm Road
Stourton
Leeds LS10 1SD

Telephone: (0113) 254 0711
Facsimile: (0113) 271 3525
Internet: http://www.asdplc.co.uk
e-mail: customer.care@asdplc.co.uk

ASD plc · Valley Farm Road · Stourton · Leeds LS10 1SD

ASD

klöckner & co multi metal distribution

Hardy-Tortuaux SA
Agence Ile de France
1, Avenue Victor-Hugo
93126 La Courneuve Cedex

Téléphone: (1) 49 34 49 34
Télécopie: (1) 49 34 49 87

Nom
Qualité/Département

Ligne directe   Télécopie directe

Hardy-Tortuaux SA · 1, Avenue Victor-Hugo · 93126 La Courneuve Cedex

Hardy-Tortuaux

klöckner & co multi metal distribution

Date

Name
Funktion/Abteilung

Klöckner & Co AG
Neudorfer Straße 3-5
D-47057 Duisburg

Telefon: (02 03) 307 0
Telefax: (02 03) 307 5000
Telex: 8 55 180

Klöckner & Co AG · Neudorfer Straße 3-5 · D-47057 Duisburg

Ein Unternehmen der VIAG-Gruppe

klöckner & co

multi metal distribution

Ihr Schreiben vom   Ihr Zeichen   Telefon-Direktwahl   Telefax-Direktwahl   Unser Zeichen   Duisburg

Vorsitzender des Aufsichtsrats:
Maximilian Ardelt
Vorstand:
Dr. Helmut Burmester (Vorsitzender)
Raimund Müsers
Carl-Heinrich Graf v. Pückler
Walter v. Szcytnicki
Michael Hütten

Sitz der Gesellschaft:
Duisburg
Handelsregister:
Amtsgericht Duisburg HRB 6902

Siège Social
173-179, Boulevard Félix-Faure
93537 Aubervilliers cedex

klöckner & co
multi metal distribution

ASD
 multi metal distribution

Namasco
klöckner & co multi metal distribution

Hardy-Tortuaux
klöckner & co multi metal distribution

Klöckner Aluminium Service
klöckner & co multi metal distribution

'Marks have a life of their own, but begin to talk to you after a while'
Lee Coomber

the assessment

The second phase was developing an international courier service, mainly out of London, and again HGV were invited to do the design work. Brochures and mail shots were again the main line of approach, and again the simplicity of the offer was reinforced by the directness of the design, although a blue cover was used for the brochure.

Upping the temperature

CLIENT

Lec
Bognor Regis, UK.

DESIGNERS

Grey Matter Williams & Phoa
London, UK.

PRODUCT/SERVICE

Refrigerator manufacturers

the background

The British refrigerator manufacturer Lec was very successful in the low-price refrigerator market when it was acquired by a Malaysian group four years ago. The new owners realised that there was an under-exploited equity in the name, especially in the export market, and asked the London-based design group Grey Matter (now Grey Matter Williams and Phoa) to advise them.

It was clear that the company's success was related to its products pricing: Lec dominated the UK market for inexpensive fridges, but even so was at the mercy of its main customers, the retail chains. To escape from this situation it was necessary to create a product and a brand that would sell on quality as well as just price. Such a change would be major, with long term consequences. Refrigerators have working lives of twenty years, and refrigerator making equipment a useful life of thirty years. Evaluating and planning the change carefully was a prime requirement. This was not only a manufacturing issue, it also concerned the image of the company, for if there was no perceived continuity between the older and new product ranges, the products would risk failing. For example, a company making breakfast cereals could easily diversify into tea and coffee, but would find it harder moving into packet soups or frozen vegetables, because the equity values in the company would be relevant to one but not the other.

The client's decision to move its product range upmarket not only involved developing a new logo, but a redefined corporate culture to make the change work right through the organisation. This was achieved by an analysis of the associations and territory of the product offer.

the research

To enable Lec to assess their current values and to see how to move forward, Grey Matter used a system of their own devising called TABS. Imagine a square divided into four equal squares by a horizontal and vertical line. Sean O'Flynn of Grey Matter explains. 'Above the horizontal is the macrocosm, below the microcosm, or, if you prefer the world above and the product below. The top left square is, standing for territory, the top right is A, for associations. Bottom left is B, for base delivery, bottom right S for satisfaction. The product of the brand - and in this case and many others they are indissoluble - has to fit into each category in ways which relate to each other completely and coherently.' O'Flynn cites a major brand such as Coca-Cola or Malboro. Malboro defines its territory and the associations very clearly: open space, freedom, the American way. This is supported by the base delivery on the pack, the mountain shape, the primary colours and the typography. And the satisfaction of this territory: the kind of smoke, the taste and bite of the cigarette, is unique to Marlboro and reinforces the expectations created by the territory and its associations.

The TABS system has three advantages. Firstly it provides in-house a complete model for approaching a brand or identity design of any kind. Secondly it provides a way of analysing the design process and solution with the client, in terms that are not design-specific. 'With some clients,' Stuart Serjent of Grey Matter explains, 'we explain the TABS concept at the start and apply it together. In others we work from the results. We are not asking the client "what do you want your logo to look like?", we are asking "what sort of company do you want to be?" The first is not the kind of question they can often answer anyway, while the second is central to the company's approach to its products and its markets.' The third advantage of TABS is that the results it produces can be tested objectively, either during the design process or at the end. And because the system has such a broad base, it can be used as a vehicle for wider changes in the company, not just to get a new brand or image.

In the case of Lec, the territory of the refrigerator can be described in shorthand as the kitchen, with its associated values of food and family, and also there are the specific associations of the refrigerator with freshness and safety. But there was an immediate difference between the design of fridges – white, square metal boxes with applied badges in gold or silver – and the ideal kitchen. Most of the fitted kitchens sold in the UK were country style kitchens in plain or varnished pine: a contradiction to the white box, though the white box also signified purity and safety. So the challenge was to move the white box closer to the ideal kitchen, without sacrificing its existing, valid associations. The existing associations could be termed strength, reliability, safety and taste, and in creating the brand image these needed to be extended to embrace sensuality and pleasure. 'Our aim was to make people say I love my fridge', as Sean O'Flynn puts it. In marketing terms, such a change could be seen as consumers deciding positively on the basis of preference, not negatively on the basis of price, so moving Lec away from its dependence on price alone as a market factor.

If the base delivery had to be a more sensual shape, how was satisfaction to be defined in terms of a refrigerator? Basically a fridge is a container: what it delivers is the condition of its contents. Fresh, clean, crisp, cool: the descriptors are all sensory terms. These qualities had to be built into the branding as well as into the product.

THE NEW IDENTITY
WAS NOT JUST
A MARK BUT A
DEFINITION OF A
NEW SET OF
PRODUCT VALUES

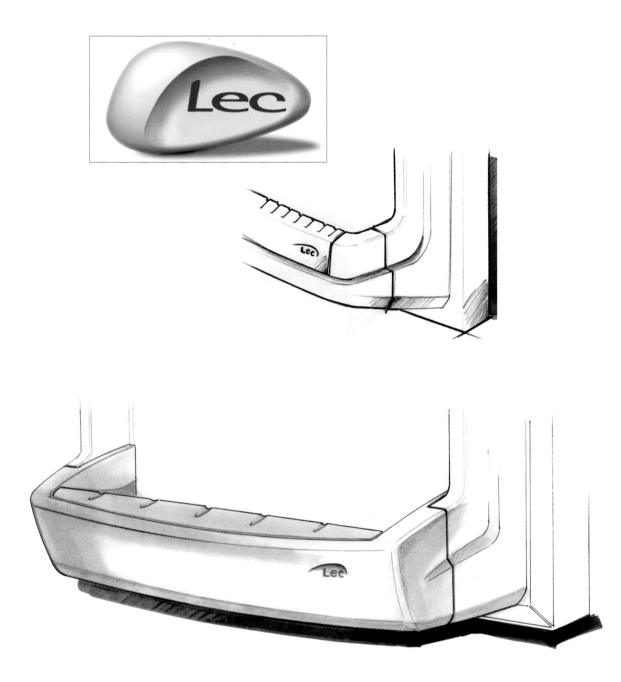

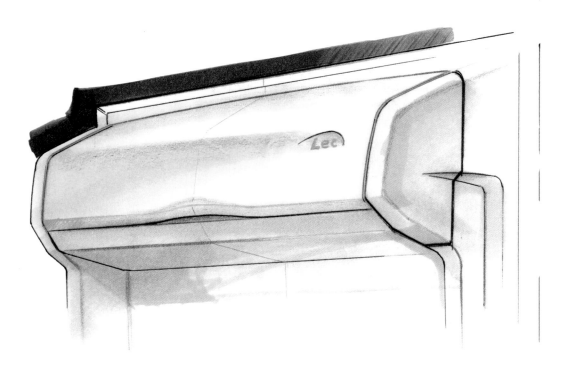

DESIGN DRAWINGS HELPED
INTEGRATE THE IDENTITY INTO
THE PRODUCT RATHER THAN
ONLY APPLYING IT

the solution

As a logo, Grey Matter evolved what they call a pebble, a sculpted asymmetrical shape engraved with the letters Lec in green sloping type. A pebble, because a pebble is natural, solid and sensual. The white colour echoed the concept of purity, the green a consciousness of the natural world. Engraved lettering because the marque is integral, not applied. This final logic is taken a step further: while the pebble mark is used on labelling, letterheads, literature and advertising, it does not appear on the fridge itself. Because, as Serjent points out, 'the pebble is not on the fridge because the fridge is also the pebble.' The brand and the product fuse into one entity. The values of the brand are the values of the product are the values of the company. And in rebuilding the brand around the new product range, Grey Matter also rebuilt the company, since the strategies for marketing and presenting a new product and a new image had to be different. 'Change can be aspirational as well as necessary.' as O'Flynn points out.

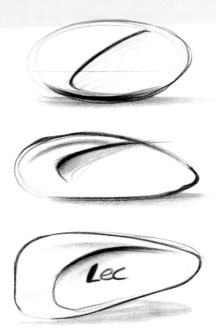

THROUGH THE TOTAL INTEGRATION OF THE LOGO THE PRODUCT ITSELF BECOMES THE BRAND

MOOD IMAGES WERE AN
IMPORTANT PART OF THE
PROCESS OF EDUCATING
MANAGEMENT ABOUT THE
COMPANY'S NEW VALUES

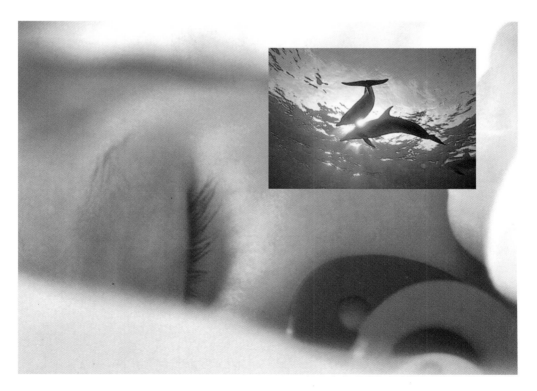

'We didn't redesign the logo, we redesigned the company'
Sean O'Flynn

the assessment

If one measure of success if the reaction of the competition, it seems like Lec got it right. A year after they introduced their new range of sculpted white refrigerators, their competitors presented new rounded shapes or coloured finishes. But if the analysis Grey Matter has done is correct, Lec will ride out the competition, since the tabs system goes beyond the immediate design brief into a range of wider issues, and so consolidates the design solution not just as a temporary visual fix or an elegant aesthetic device, but as a tool with a logic that runs into the raison d'etre of the client company itself. Grey Matter are unusual, among design companies, in developing and using such a formal model: others arrive at similar conclusion by experience or intuition. But Grey Matter have accepted the necessity for design companies to work alongside their clients, and see the design result as part of a wider strategy for the client.

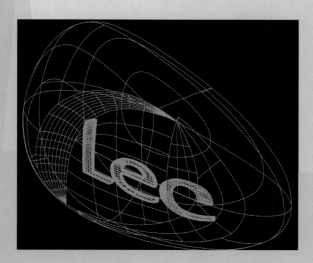

Good moves

CLIENT

Esprit Europe
London, UK.

DESIGNERS

HGV
London, UK.

PRODUCT/SERVICE

Courier services

the background

The Eurostar high-speed rail service links London to Paris and Brussels through the Channel Tunnel. With up to ten trains a day to and from each destination, the service offers a comfortable and rapid city centre to city centre passenger service. But as the trains also have some freight capacity, the parent company, London and Continental Railways, decided to add a courier service, using the trains to offer, initially, a same-day or overnight delivery between the three capital cities. Three design companies were invited to make a non-creative pitch for both naming the company and designing its identity, which was won by the London-based group HGV.

esprit *europe*

the brief

The initial brief was for an identity for a courier service using the high-speed train link under the English Channel. With the success of the first venture, the brief was extended to a wider range of services, through a series of related promotional brochures and packages.

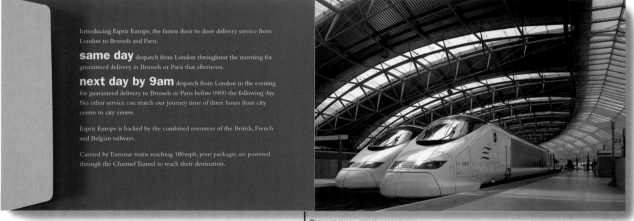

Introducing Esprit Europe, the fastest door to door delivery service from London to Brussels and Paris.

same day despatch from London throughout the morning for guaranteed delivery in Brussels or Paris that afternoon.

next day by 9am despatch from London in the evening for guaranteed delivery to Brussels or Paris before 0900 the following day. No other service can match our journey time of three hours from city centre to city centre.

Esprit Europe is backed by the combined resources of the British, French and Belgian railways.

Carried by Eurostar trains reaching 186mph, your packages are powered through the Channel Tunnel to reach their destination.

PROMOTIONAL ITEMS, CAREFULLY TARGETED, WERE ESSENTIAL TO DEVELOPING AWARENESS OF THE SERVICES OFFERED

the solution

The first task was the name: here there were two main factors emerging from the brief. The name had to be comprehensible across the three languages, and contain the European concept. Esprit Europe achieved this: the words read in all three languages (English, French and Flemish), and the assonances of the term echo those of Eurostar. The logo, too, was influenced by the Eurostar connection: an outline parcel with a sloping front (to echo the distinctive streamline of the Eurostar locomotive), a touch repeated in the italic sans serif lower case lettering of the name.

the **development**

But Esprit was, at first, a courier company only serving three cities, while competing with the likes of UPS, Fedex and DHL. Esprit had the advantage of offering a same day service, but certainly there was no budget for television or other broadband advertising. Instead, HGV devised a series of carefully targeted mail shots, using simple brochures printed with brown paper covers, like parcels. The delivery vans were also painted brown with mock labels on the side panels. Clients would find a copy of that day's Le Figaro newspaper from Paris waiting on their desk in the morning (Le Monde, the other French paper of record, is published in the afternoon) with a brown paper wrapper with the Esprit logo and the words 'News Travels Fast'. Or a packet of Belgian chocolates labelled 'Fast Food'.

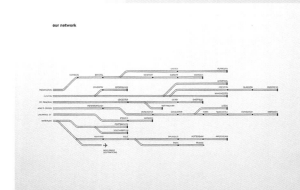

AS NEW SERVICES DEVELOPED,
NEW PRESENTATIONS
WERE NEEDED

'The colour and material on its own was saying "Esprit" in the same way that pink newspaper says Financial Times.'
Pierre Vermier

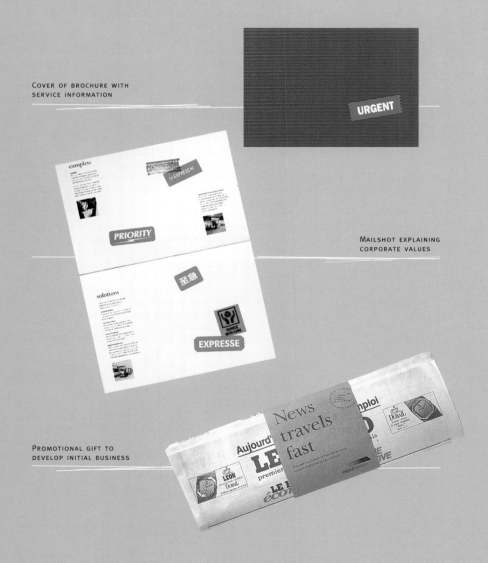

COVER OF BROCHURE WITH
SERVICE INFORMATION

MAILSHOT EXPLAINING
CORPORATE VALUES

PROMOTIONAL GIFT TO
DEVELOP INITIAL BUSINESS

VEHICLE LIVERY AND
ADVERTISING MAINTAINED
THE ORIGINAL BROWN PAPER
PARCEL PROPOSITION

A response rate of up to ten percent on a mailing shot is generally considered average. Esprit was getting take-up rates of over eighty percent. The design and marketing mix was perfect. From the design standpoint, the proposition was a simple one: 'this is what Esprit can do - same day to Paris and Brussels; this is how - using Eurostar; these are the times and charges.' This information was elegantly but simply set out, in a no-nonsense way. Esprit built its business from nothing in 1995 to a turnover of £400,000 in just five months.

The second phase was developing an international courier service, mainly out of London, and again HGV was invited to do the design work. Brochures and mail shots were again the main line of approach, and again the simplicity of the offer was reinforced by the directness of the design, and although a blue cover was used for the brochure the continuity was maintained (and the formality of the pages reduced) by using white on red 'urgent' or 'priority' stickers as in the original brochures and mailshots. When it came to the third phase, extending the service across the United Kingdom, HGV realised that the parcel motif had, in customer's eyes, become an integral part of the logo. Therefore it went back to the brown paper approach for the brochure for the UK service.

the assessment

The different developments of Esprit were unexpected: HGV thought it would bow out after the initial set-up, but in fact has stayed involved fairly continuously for four years. This is partly due to the success of the business, but that success was in part achieved through developing initially a design proposal that was sufficiently direct and well crafted to reach its target market, and robust enough to provide a design platform for the subsequent development of the business.

Flying the World, not Flying the Flag

CLIENT

British Airways
London, England

DESIGNERS

Newell & Sorrell
London, England

PRODUCT/SERVICE

Airline

the background

The idea of aircraft as flag carriers dates in part from the early history of commercial aviation, when sea transport was the nearest form of international trade that could provide an organisational model, and in part from the last days of empires, when countries needed a secure means of transport for diplomats and officials, and for mail services. With the need to rebuild commercial airline services in Europe after the Second World War, many airlines became nationalised, and so identified with the country of origin and ownership. British Airways was created by the merger in the 1970's of the pre-war British Overseas Airways Corporation and British European Airways. Both had established identities, BEA's built around its successful 'We Fly the Flag' advertising strapline, BOAC's on its Speedbird logo, dating from 1938. But times change, and perceptions change. The airline is now a publicly quoted corporation, and was looking to redefine its position in a changing commercial environment.

The standard approach to a national airline identity is to link it strongly with national elements: Alitalia uses the green red and white of the Italian flag, KLM a crown motif as a reminder that the Netherlands is a monarchy (the KLM translates as Royal Dutch Airline), Air Canada a maple leaf. And the normal practice is to use the chosen motif with a maximum of consistency in order to reinforce its message. According to this view, any distraction from the corporate statement is a dilution of its efficiency.

BRITISH AIRWAYS

the brief

The design of a new identity for one of the world's largest airlines was based on four years of research and preparation, and breaks with traditional identity rules to create a bold global image based not on a single logo but a series of related designs from around the world, together with a softer approach to the treatment of the corporate name, so positioning British Airways as 'global and

BRITISH AIRWAYS

BRITISH AIRWAYS

the research

The detailed logic behind the decision to redesign the corporate identity stems from a major investigation launched by British Airways in 1994, to study the future development of the airline, and to understand and analyse public perceptions of it, nationally and internationally, and among passengers and non-passengers. The case for a new identity emerged from this process, which defined British Airways as being 'global and caring'. What this superficially simple phase meant was that British Airways was a diverse community of people based in Britain, providing a service to the communities of the world. It did not mean putting Britain or Britons first, it was not about dominating the airways, it was not about power and success except in terms of having the ability to satisfy the needs of the customers. There is a deliberate contrast here with other airlines whose offers are either based on some skewed notion of supremacy or of exclusivity, or of authority. Nor is it a populist or somehow downmarket position. The opposite is dictatorial, after all. is not weak but democratic.

The new British Airways World Images logo/branding unveiled in June 1997 was the result of two year's close collaboration between BA's design management department, headed by Chris Holt, and their selected designers Interbrand Newell and Sorrell. The new identity, as far as the treatment of the name is concerned, comprises a softer typographical style, a new Speedmarque ribbon logo, and a colour scheme closer to Britain's traditional red, white and blue. To this is added a series of images representing the creative work of different peoples and places. For Interbrand Newell and Sorrell took the global concept not in a simply geographical and political sense but as a network of communities who are served by the airline. From this concept of patterns the idea of World Images was born. As John Sorrell points out, 'World Images is not about only identifying BA as the national flag carrier. Our task was to position BA as a world brand, the equivalent of Coke or Microsoft, but one which is based and has its roots in Britain.'

UNION FLAG
UNITED KINGDOM

POTTERY
ENGLAND

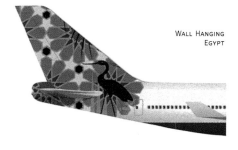

WALL HANGING
EGYPT

WOOD CARVING
NORTH AMERICA

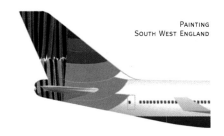

PAINTING
SOUTH WEST ENGLAND

TRADITIONAL PAINTING
JAPAN

CERAMIC PANEL
GERMANY

CELTIC CALLIGRAPHY
IRELAND

SEVEN JACKALS
UNDER TREES IN
THE KALAHARI
PAINTED BY
CGOISE

the **solution**

The largest identity surface, the 60 foot high tailfin of a Boeing 747, is not given over to a single logo or image but to a selected image among the thirty-three 'World Images', abstract or semi-abstract patterns created by living artists whose work represents continuity between creative, real and active communities (ignoring national boundaries, be it said). When the roll-out of the identity is complete in the year 2000, each aircraft in the BA fleet will have one of the World Images on its tailfin, and the images will also be used on business cards, corporate publications and documents: more images, with time, will be added to the repertory. No way either that work by a Dutch artist is going to be seen only on the Schipol/Heathrow route. Ideally the planespotters of Amsterdam are going to see a series of different World Images, from Japan or India, St Ives or Nairobi.

The selection process that led to the choice of Interbrand Newell and Sorrell was a complex one: one consultancy was used to assess potential candidates worldwide, a second one made a blind approach to a first list of forty, asking for a credentials presentation, and only then did BA invite a final shortlist of four design teams to make an initial, paid presentation. As Chris Holt says 'we chose Interbrand Newell & Sorrell on the basis of their skills and their vision. We developed the World Images idea from an element in their presentation to us, but which was part of the background briefing, not a formal proposal, originally inspired by the idea of world patterns made by humankind throughout our evolution.'

The concept of serving a global community is reinforced by a collection of images called 'People Photography', which showed the ordinary citizens of the world in their communities. It gave a human context to the World Image series, and so underpinned the new identity. The 'People Photography' images are used in direct marketing, promotions and other below-the-line applications. Extending an identity in this way shows how closely related the launch of a new identity needs to be with the marketing and overall presentation of a company's services. It creates an added depth to the image of the company, and strengthens the perception of the company culture, thus enabling the transition to a 'world brand' as suggested by John Sorrell.

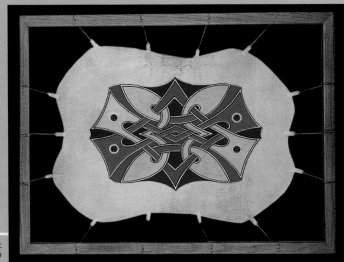

Contemporary Celtic
illumination by Irish
artist Timothy O'Neill

BRITISH
AIRWAYS

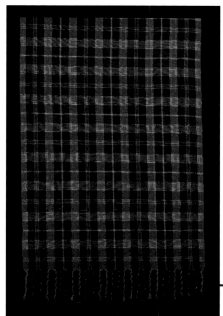

MODERN SCOTTISH
TARTAN WOVEN BY
PETER MACDONALD

the assessment

Because of its technical complexities, airline corporate identities have tended to be the preserve of a small group of companies with established track records. The fact that Interbrand Newell & Sorrell was a newcomer worked to its advantage, in that more experienced designers might have rejected some of its ideas before starting to develop them. Putting a design on an aircraft's tailfin, for example, involves painting individual colours through masks made by hand, complex enough in itself, but it has also to be integrated into the servicing schedule of the aircraft.

When BOAC introduced Indian stewardesses to its long haul routes in the 1950's, it made haste to explain to the travelling public that Norman Hartnell (fashion designer in ordinary to HM the Queen) had been consulted over the choice of clothing colours. Since then, BA (as it became) has grown, and grown up. Its decision to state its international role so boldly sends a message to designers everywhere looking at what have traditionally been seen as national brands. They are perhaps missing a much larger and very important point.

To my mind the success of the World Images concept is not only that it defines a global activity through concepts of communities not through concepts of nationality, nor is it that it avoids the clichés of much corporate identity work with such elegance. The subtlety of the solution lies in pairing the series of images, with their endlessly different cultural resonances, with the relaxed yet ordered Speedmarque, name and colours. And the pleasure in it stems from the variety. For many people flying today is a matter of routine: any sense of excitement or adventure flying may have once had has been worn down by sameness and repetition. World Images shifts that forgotten perception back into focus. The sight of an exotic design on the tailfin as you are waiting in the departure lounge to board is a gentle reminder that you can actually go wherever you want. And the next time you take the same business flight to the same destination, there will be a different image waiting for you.

The four key elements

the conclusion

What is the role of the designer? If the logo is the base element in the corporate or brand identity, and the corporate or brand identity the base element in the corporate or brand culture, then clearly the way to approach the design or redesign of a logo, identity or brand is from the top down. Understanding the corporate culture first will give the necessary framework to even the most specific brief, and help define possible solutions later, as well as excluding inappropriate options at an early stage. The overriding question to put to the client is therefore 'what sort of company do you want your company to be?'

In approaching the task in this way, it becomes clear that researching the brief is of primary importance, whether this research is conducted through formal market research methods or a design audit or through informal discussions with the client and others. Such discussions can be visually based, as with the TABS system used by Grey Matter, described on page 122, but their normal goal is to establish a vocabulary or just a list of key terms, that describe the company's values and aspirations. The value of such an approach, for the directors and managers of a company, is that it enables them to follow and understand the design process from a familiar standpoint, rather than considering visual options for which they may have no wider context, apart from personal preference.

Once this research period is well under way, then the designer's visual skills have something to work on. A successful design will be the visual expression of the corporate or brand values uncovered by the research. It has often been said that good design delivers a solution beyond the client's expectations. The real truth in this is that good design is based on a clear understanding of the client's expectations and ambitions, and visually presents a solution that the client could not have devised or imagined alone.

When Hutchison Telecommunications decided to launch a mobile phone network in the UK, they asked Wolff Olins to advise them on both the identity and the name for the service. There were already two established networks in the UK, and mobile phone usage was beginning to trickle down' from business use to private use. Wolff Olins research confirmed that mobile phone usage was set to spread rapidly, and suggested that the positioning of the existing companies was based on the concept of the mobile phone as new technology. But the new market of private users would not be interested in the technology, just in the service, and so to base the new offer on technology would be neither relevant nor original. In fact Wolff Olins went a step further, and envisaged the mobile phone as becoming, in a short time, as common a piece of personal equipment as a Walkman or an electronic bank card. In other words it needed to be presented as a lifestyle object, not just in terms of communication or technics. They therefore chose the name Orange for the company, and developed guidelines for presenting the corporate image that were based on the use of mobile phones not as exclusive or complex, but as absolutely straightforward and contemporary. The name deliberately had no associations with the telephone business (which was a useful feature in a teaser advertising campaign before the product launch).

The result of Wolff Olins understanding of the changing perception of mobile phones (from yuppie toys to everyday objects) made Orange an immediate and continuing success, despite its apparently arbitrary nature and its apparent failure to play by the rules' and position itself within the established mobile phone market. In fact, its success came from putting itself outside that market, but into the future marketplace for the product.

'Designers should read about everything except design'
Philippe Starck

Among the books consulted during the writing of this book or relevant to the study of identity and branding are

Bak, Per **How Nature Works** (Oxford, 1997)

Barthes, Roland **Mythologies** (Editions du Seuil, 1957)

Bayley, Stephen **Coke!** (Boilerhouse, 1986)

Berger, John **Ways of Seeing** (Penguin, 1976)

Blaich, Robert & Janet **Product Design and Corporate Strategy** (McGraw Hill, 1994)

Dormer, Peter **Design since 1945** (Thames & Hudson, 1993)

Haks, Frans I **Menhir: Atelier Mendini** (Edizioni L'Archivolto, 1997)

Heskett, John **Philips** (Trefoil, 1989)

Kicherer, Sybille, **Olivetti** (Trefoil, 1990)

Loewy, Raymond **Industrial Design** (Overlook Press, 1979)

Lorenz, Christopher **The Design Dimension** (Blackwell, 1986)

Nouvel, Jean, ed. **International Design Yearbook 1995** (Laurence King 1995)

Olins, Wally **Corporate Identity** (Thames & Hudson, 1991)

Olins, Wally & Morgan, Conway Lloyd **International Corporate Identity 1** (Laurence King, 1995)

Starck (Taschen, 1995)

Tanizaki, Junichiro **Eloge de l'ombre** (PUF, 1988)

Virilio, Paul **Bunker Archéologie** (CCI, 1976)

the designers

Grey Matter Williams & Phoa, London

HGV, London

Lewis Moberly, London

Lippa Pearce, Richmond

MetaDesign, Berlin

Newell & Sorrell, London

Nike Design Studio, New York

Northcross, Edinburgh

Pentagram, New York

Pentagram, London

Philips CID, Eindhoven

Rage Design, West Wycombe

Paul Rand, New York

Springpoint, London

Studio Starck, Issy-Les-Moulineaux

Wolff Olins, London

the clients

Ballet-Tech, New York

Birds Eye, Walton-on-Thames

British Airways, Heathrow

Cearns & Brown, Shipley

Coca Cola, Atlanta

Direct Line, Croydon, England

Dusseldorf Airport, Dusseldorf

Esprit Europe, London

Hong Kong Airport Core Programme, Hong Kong

IBM, White Plains, NY

International Distillers, London

Klöckner & Co, Duisburg, Germany

Lawyers Committee on Human Rights, New York

Lec, Bognor Regis

OAO, Brussels

Oxygen, Vienna

Savoy Hotels Group, London

Techniquest, Cardiff

Wineworld, London

the activities

Business services

Charities

Consumer goods

Education

Food and drink

Government organisations

Leisure

Manufacturing